Theodore M. Shaw, former director-counsel and president of the
NAACP Legal Defense and Educational Fund, is the Julius L. Cham-
bers Distinguished Professor of Law and Director of the Center for
Civil Rights at the University of North Carolina School of Law at
Chapel Hill, where he lives.

THE FERGUSON REPORT

DEPARTMENT OF JUSTICE INVESTIGATION OF THE FERGUSON POLICE DEPARTMENT

UNITED STATES DEPARTMENT OF JUSTICE,
CIVIL RIGHTS DIVISION

Introduction by

THEODORE M. SHAW

THE NEW PRESS

NEW YORK
LONDON

Requests for permission to reproduce selections from this book should be mailed to:
Permissions Department, The New Press, 120 Wall Street, 31st floor, New York, NY 10005.

Published in the United States by The New Press, New York, 2015.
Distributed by Perseus Distribution

LIBRARY OF CONGRESS CATALOGING-IN-PUBLICATION DATA

The Ferguson report : Department of Justice investigation of the Ferguson Police Department /
United States Department of Justice, Civil Rights Division; introduction by Theodore M. Shaw.
    pages cm
  ISBN 978-1-62097-160-4 (paperback) — ISBN 978-1-62097-165-9 (e-book) 1. Ferguson (Mo.).
Police Department. 2. Discrimination in criminal justice administration—Ferguson—Missouri.
3. Police-community relations—Missouri—Ferguson. 4. Police—Complaints against—Missouri—
Ferguson. I. Shaw, Theodore M. II. United States. Department of Justice.
  HV8148.F47F47 2015
  364.1'3230977865—dc23
                                    2015015187

The New Press publishes books that promote and enrich public discussion and understanding of the issues vital to our democracy and to a more equitable world. These books are made possible by the enthusiasm of our readers; the support of a committed group of donors, large and small; the collaboration of our many partners in the independent media and the not-for-profit sector; booksellers, who often hand-sell New Press books; librarians; and above all by our authors.

www.thenewpress.com

Book design and composition by Bookbright Media

Printed in the United States of America

10 9 8 7 6 5 4 3 2 1

CONTENTS

INTRODUCTION

THEODORE M. SHAW

WHILE MOST FATAL SHOOTINGS OF UNARMED BLACK PEOPLE DO NOT
lead to uprisings, riots, or rebellions, for decades now, almost every major
urban uprising or "race riot" in the United States has begun with an interac-
tion, often fatal, between a black man and the police. The Harlem race riot
of 1964, the 1965 Watts race riot, the 1967 Newark race riot, the 1980 Liberty City, Florida, race riot, the 1992 Rodney King riot in Los Angeles, the
1996 St. Petersburg, Florida, race riot, the 2001 Cincinnati race riot, and the
protests following the killing of Oscar Grant in Oakland in 2009 all started
the same way. As we prepared to go to press, with the death of Freddie
Gray, Baltimore became yet another city that has erupted in violence following allegations of excessive force against black men by law enforcement.

In August 2015 a policeman in the St. Louis suburb of Ferguson, Missouri, shot and killed an eighteen-year-old, unarmed black man. As con-
flicting versions of the event circulated through the majority black town,
tensions escalated. Aided by social media and amplified by the twenty-four
hour news cycle, news from Ferguson flashed across the nation and around
the world. In the hours, days, weeks, and months that followed the death
of Michael Brown at the hands of Officer Darren Wilson, protest ensued,
mostly peaceful but some violent enough to have become known as the
Ferguson riots.

Ferguson did not happen in a vacuum. Police killings of unarmed individuals are, unfortunately, not uncommon. While the facts of each case are

different, there is a numbing familiarity when an unarmed black boy, teenager, or man is killed by a police officer. A well-worn script often unfolds in the aftermath of each death: The police officer recounts a threat to his life, which allegedly includes a weapon. The dead black man is dehumanized and demonized through the release of any record of past wrongdoing in an attempt to implant the worthy-of-death notion in the public's mind. In most instances, state and local authorities do not bring charges against the officer. In the rare circumstance when there is an indictment, the officer is, more often than not, cleared of wrongdoing. In many cases the family of the decedent and community activists seek federal review and prosecution, usually without success. For the families of the unarmed dead, there is rarely any semblance of justice.

Many black people are bone weary and cynical about a broken criminal justice system that is quick to incarcerate individuals from their communities, even while it countenances the harassment and even the killing of unarmed individuals by law enforcement. A black woman, Marissa Alexander of Jacksonville, Florida, unsuccessfully invoked Florida's "stand your ground" law and was sentenced to twenty years in prison for firing a warning shot, allegedly in defense against an abusive husband; George Zimmerman, a "neighborhood watch" volunteer, successfully invoked Florida's "stand your ground" law to allow him to kill unarmed, seventeen-year-old Trayvon Martin with impunity.

The survivors of the unarmed and innocent dead include a bereaved network of mothers and fathers, sisters and brothers, widows and girlfriends, widowers and boyfriends, and children. Some have become involuntary activists who, long before Michael Brown died in Ferguson, ceaselessly voiced anguish over the deaths of their unarmed loved ones and pursued a seemingly futile quest for justice. Others live with a dull ache and a hole in their spirits and in their hearts, dug by the despair that is the child of hopelessness.

While the Justice Department has investigated excessive force in a number of police departments, what may distinguish Ferguson is the fact that on March 4, 2015, the United States Department of Justice, Civil Rights Division, issued a 102-page report on policing in Ferguson[1]. The report is comprehensive, objective, factual, and damning. *Investigation of the Ferguson Police Department* illuminates a municipality that is dependent on practices and policies that criminalize its majority black populations through traffic violations, municipal ordinances, false arrests, charging practices, and impositions of penalties for petty violations and charges that lead to debt and imprisonment. As the Department of Justive report concluded: 1) "Ferguson's police and municipal court practices both reflect and exacerbate existing racial bias, including racial stereotypes"; 2) "Ferguson's own data establish clear racial disparities that adversely impact African Americans"; and 3) "[t]he evidence shows that discriminatory intent is part of the reason for these disparities."[2] In summary, the Ferguson Report reveals a pattern or practice of unlawful conduct within the Ferguson Police Department that violates the First, Fourth, and Fourteenth amendments to the United States Constitution, and federal statutory law. Over the years there have been a number of investigations and reports on the causes of and events surrounding racial violence in American communities; the Ferguson report stands out both for its comprehensive detail and as a twenty-first century reminder that we have not left this kind of unrest in our rearview mirror.

The events in Ferguson in the summer of 2014 were bigger than Michael Brown and Darren Wilson. And the Ferguson protests ignited a multiracial campaign, if not a movement, captured in the refrain "Black Lives Matter," reminding us of a long, sordid history of violence by private actors and law enforcement against African Americans and the devaluation of black lives, stretching from slavery and reconstruction to the present.

In 1944 the Swedish sociologist Gunnar Myrdal, in his classic study of race in America, *An American Dilemma*, wrote that he was convinced that "the Southern police system . . . represents a crucial and strategic factor in race relations."[3] Myrdal wrote that "the most publicized type of police brutality is the extreme case of Negroes being killed by policemen."[4] Seventy years later, these observations remain sadly true, even in the wake of the Ferguson report. Mere months after the report's initial release the nation was bombarded by the video of the shooting death of Walter Scott in North Charleston, South Carolina, shot in the back by a policeman after a traffic stop.

But going beyond these "extreme" cases, and citing sociologist Arthur Raper, Myrdal further identified a more insidious force at work: "the dynamics of the fee system," in which "all the minor court officials, and in some instances the prosecuting attorneys get their pay out of fines."[5] "This system," Myrdal explained, ". . . puts a premium upon making those arrests and getting those convictions which will yield fees and costs without jeopardizing the political popularity of the fee-getting officials."[6]

There is an element of common corruption that preys upon the vulnerable in a manner that may not be driven solely by considerations of race, but by a kind of venality that, when combined with the racial prejudices of municipal employees, including the police and court system, is both banal and toxic. In Ferguson, the Department of Justice found just such a toxic combination, concluding that "over time, Ferguson's police and municipal court practices have sown deep mistrust between parts of the community and the police department, undermining law enforcement legitimacy among African Americans in particular."[7] In a perfect illustration of Myrdal's "fee system," the Ferguson report found that:

> Ferguson's law enforcement practices are shaped by the City's focus on revenue rather than by public safety needs. This emphasis on revenue has compromised the institutional character of Ferguson's police department, contributing to a pattern of unconstitutional policing and has also shaped its municipal court, leading to procedures that raise due process concerns and inflict unnecessary harms on members of the Ferguson community.

The report continued,

> Partly as a result of City and [Ferguson Police Department] priorities, many officers appear to see some residents, espe-

cially those who live in Ferguson's predominantly African-American neighborhoods, less as constituents to be protected than as potential offenders and sources of revenue.[8]

Ferguson, Missouri, as it turns out, is Myrdal's "fee system" on steroids.

Ironically, on the same date that it released *Investigation of the Ferguson Police Department*, the Department of Justice released a second, 86-page report, on the Michael Brown shooting itself.[9] The Michael Brown report found no basis on which to disagree with the decision by local prosecutors to clear Police Officer Darren Wilson of all local charges, or on which to bring federal charges against Officer Wilson. For reasons detailed over the course of the report, the Department of Justice found that "Wilson's conduct in shooting Brown as [Brown] advanced on Wilson, and until he fell to the ground, was not objectively unreasonable and thus not a violation of 18 U.S.C. Sec. 242"[10].

Many people were disappointed in the Department of Justice's conclusion that it could not pursue federal charges. And not everyone feels compelled to wait until the dust clears and the facts are determined. For those who are familiar with the applicable federal law in Officer Wilson's case, however, the Department of Justice's conclusion was not a surprise. I have been a civil and human rights lawyer for thirty-five years. As an African American, I share in the grief, frustration, and anger each time the life of an unarmed black person is lost as a consequence of excessive force wielded by police. As a lawyer, though, I have learned that a rush to judgment in a specific case rarely holds up over time, and things are almost always more complicated than they first appear. We are called upon to sift through the facts, unmoved by passion, keeping an open mind until we are able to arrive at as objective a conclusion as possible.

In the case of Michael Brown, the law requires a showing that Officer Wilson acted "willfully," that is, "for the specific purpose of violating the law."[11] This is a high standard to meet. The officer could have used poor judgment, but that flawed judgment would not satisfy the Sec. 242 standard, which requires an adjudicator to get into the mind of the actor and prove that he took his action not just recklessly or negligently, but that he took it *for the specific purpose of violating the law.*

The fact that federal prosecutors concluded they did not have the requisite proof to support federal charges against Wilson, however, did not bar the Department of Justice's Civil Rights Division from examining the City of Ferguson's overall policing practices and policies. And the fact that the Department of Justice *did* examine those practices, in a clear-eyed and ultimately scathing way, is both historic and a cause for optimism.

Ironically, systemic issues concerning race and policing came into even more stark relief than they might have been if Wilson had been indicted. [12] The Department of Justice was free to pursue an investigation of the city, the police department, and the judicial system of the City of Ferguson in an attempt to understand the context in which the events following the shooting of Michael Brown took place. Even if Darren Wilson was not criminally indicted, in a broader sense the City of Ferguson, Missouri, stood indicted for its unconstitutional and racially discriminatory actions, deeds, and omissions in its daily treatment of its African-American citizens.

The killing of Michael Brown fell into a deep and ancient American fault line. Race has always been America's deepest dilemma, and it remains so today, even in "The Age of Obama." Maybe especially in "The Age of Obama." Many Americans believe that black people are collectively oversensitive, and perhaps unjustifiably paranoid, un-objective, obsessed, and even distorted in their views when it comes to race. I have come to believe that when groups of people are subjected to oppression, subordination, discrimination, collective violence, and even genocide, those experiences are "crazy-making."

When Jewish people continue to say "Never Again", and warn of a rising tide of anti-Semitism, many others often react with skepticism and hostility, especially if they perceive, rightly or wrongly, that many Jews are empowered in one way or another. Jews, however, know full well that, whatever degree of power or wealth some may have had in mid-twentieth century Germany, they were not protected against the Holocaust. They may seem paranoid, but they are not crazy.

African Americans are not crazy when they see racial discrimination and racism, although their experiences with race and racism may sometimes lead them to conclusions that are premature or misplaced. As a parent, I struggle with what to teach my children. I do not want them to walk around perceiving racial bogey-men where they do not exist. On the other hand, I do not want them to believe naively that we have reached racial nirvana, only to have them shot in the back, asphyxiated, or their spine broken by the police force paid to protect them.

Whatever the merits of any individual instance in which law enforcement kills an unarmed black person (and in recent cases, these "merits" have included allegedly stealing cigarillos, running away from a traffic stop, and running away after "making eye contact" with the police), black people are not crazy or "crying wolf" when they view law enforcement with suspicion and doubt. New York mayor Bill de Blasio, father of a biracial teenaged son, in the aftermath of the deaths of Michael Brown in Ferguson and Eric Garner in Staten Island, talked publicly about the painful wisdom regularly imparted by parents of black boys from an early age, which certainly includes counseling young black men *not* to assert their constitutional rights in encounters with the police, lest those young men end up another sad statistic. The head of New York's police union, tone deaf or blissfully steeped in ignorance and denial, charged that de Blasio "threw cops under the bus." Sadly, when law enforcement officials and union leaders dismiss legitimate concerns born out of the lived experiences of African Americans, they alienate themselves from a portion of the community they are charged to serve.

Some commentators also seem unable to distinguish between violence within populations plagued by the dysfunction endemic to concentrated poverty, on the one hand, and violence against unarmed individuals perpetrated by those charged with protecting those communities, on the other. These commentators seem to suggest that African Americans forfeit the right to protest police brutality because of some theory of collective responsibility for criminal behavior within black communities. Perhaps these arguments are intended to be a distraction. Taken at their word, however, those who advance such arguments reveal a poverty of thoughtfulness that should disqualify them from serious public discourse.

To be sure, policing is a difficult and often dangerous job. The tragic shooting deaths by a mentally ill assailant of two New York City police officers, allegedly in retaliation for Michael Brown's death, underscored that reality. In the demonstrations following Michael Brown's death some news outlets reported that some protesters explicitly called for violence and police officers' deaths. It should hardly seem necessary for people with legitimate concerns about police misconduct to have to condemn the deeds of individuals who advocate or perpetrate violence against police officers.

But while it is wrong for protesters to use incendiary language that calls for violence against police, it is also wrong to blame peaceful protestors, responsibly exercising their First Amendment rights, for violence against police. All law enforcement officers do not use excessive force against African Americans, and most protesters are not irresponsible in their exercise of their First Amendment rights. However, a culture within police departments of silence among good officers about excessive force on the part of other police officers, tears at the fabric of the relationship between law enforcement and the communities they police. Likewise, a failure by those protesting police brutality to condemn and distance themselves from calls for violence against police, compromises their protest.

Among the direct evidence of racial bias found in the Justice Department investigation were racist emails and other communications between court and law enforcement personnel, including crude "jokes" aimed at president Barack Obama and his wife. These crude and racist depictions of the first African American president and First Lady are the tip of an iceberg that we have glimpsed since 2008. A congressman from a state with a history of racial extremism shouts out at the State of the Union Address, calling the President of the United States a liar. A governor of a western state deigns to lecture the President of the United States on the tarmac of an airport, wagging her finger in his face as if he were not the highest office holder in the land. The Senate minority leader, upon Barack Obama's election as president, announces as his number one priority, in a tone dripping with hostility, at a time of great financial crisis and during a war on terrorism, his goal of ensuring that the president would be unsuccessful, setting out on a path of political obstruction that surpasses anything in living memory. A chief judge of a federal district court circulates racist jokes by email, including one about bestiality and the president's mother. A New England sheriff calls the President of the United States the "n" word and although the sheriff is forced to resign, he refuses to apologize. A former big city mayor with a history of disdain for African Americans, who never saw a killing of an unarmed black man by a policeman he did not defend, engages in a tirade against the president that drips with disdain and criticism over the president's concern about Ferguson. The list goes on and on.

In the story of Ferguson lies the great contradiction of "The Age of Obama." In "post-racial" America, racism is alive and well. The glow that accompanied Barack Obama's election in 2008 is long gone. Its power was in the fact that with the election of the first African-American president it appeared that we had overcome America's greatest demon. But that impression was only a partial reality. The United States *has* crossed a Rubicon. The election and re-election of President Obama signaled an irrevocable turning point in American history, partly attributable to changing attitudes among white Americans, and partly to changing demographics. Yet the election of Barack Obama has unleashed forces of reaction and racism that are reflected in the racist jokes, disrespect, and disdain directed at the First Family and at African Americans more generally. Black people see it and feel it, as do many other Americans. Ferguson, Missouri, embodies all of these forces, some subterranean and many undisguised. These are dying gasps and political convulsions on the part of an old order that will not pass easily from the American stage.

Some years ago I took a taxi from Detroit's airport to Ann Arbor with a young man from Wales. I shared with him that I was a civil rights lawyer, and he shared with me the most unexpected thing he had learned about the United States: the persistence of race. "Race," he said of America, was "like a civil war you hold under your breath."

The United States Department of Justice *Investigation of the Ferguson Police Department*, conducted under the administration of an African-American president and an African-American attorney general, is an objective, unblinking, and factual inquiry into a twenty-first century American city caught between the past and the future. It is proof that the election of Barack Obama was a turning point in American history, but that systemic racism and inequality did not disappear the moment President Obama was elected President of the United States.

The Ferguson Report will take its place on the shelf with other important governmental reports—the 1968 *Report of the Advisory Commission on Civil Disorders*, the 1969 *Final Report of the National Commission on the Causes and Prevention of Violence*, the *Report on the Assassination of President John F. Kennedy*, the *9/11 Report of The National Commission on Terrorist Attacks Upon the United States*, and others. These reports and investigations bear silent witness to some of the most important issues of our times; the use of deadly force against unarmed African Americans remains one of those issues. The Department of Justice's scathing *Investigation of the Ferguson Police Department* deserves to be read and heeded by all Americans, so that we can begin the process of turning the tragedy of Ferguson into a turning point for our country.

Ferguson puts the lie to twenty-first-century America's claim of post-racialism. It is a reminder that our most long-lasting dilemma, the flaw that has stained our nation even before its independence and over which we fought a civil war, has not yet been consigned to the dustbin of history. Ours is a Dickensian dilemma. It is the best of times; it is the worst of times. We have a black man as President of the United States; we have black men incarcerated at historic rates, again and again killed by law enforcement while unarmed, and missing in huge proportions from the communities and families from which they come. Ferguson is the tip of an iceberg, shaped by the legacy of the slavery-to–Jim Crow continuum that even today accounts for eight out of every ten days that people of African descent have spent in what is now the United States. It reminds us that, in spite of the extraordinary progress our nation has made, we are not as far removed from that legacy as we would like to think. One of the hallmarks of American racism has been the devaluation of black lives. Out of Ferguson's tragedy and turmoil comes a protest and refrain voiced by people of all races and backgrounds: Black lives matter. Yet even after Ferguson, unarmed black men continue to die at the hands of police. The Department of Justice's report on Ferguson has not brought an end to these deaths, but it bears witness to the systemic issues that, in at least one small town, have allowed racism to flourish in the new millennium.

Notes

1. *Investigation of the Ferguson Police Department.*

2. Ibid., 2.

3. Gunnar Myrdal, *An American Dilemma* (New York: Harper & Row, 1944), 544.

4. Ibid., 542.

5. Ibid., 548.

6. Ibid.

7. *Investigation of the Ferguson Police Department*, 2.

8. Ibid.

9. *Department of Justice Report Regarding the Criminal Investigation into the Shooting Death of Michael Brown by Ferguson, Missouri Police Officer Darren Wilson.*

10. Ibid., 85.

11. Ibid., 11.

12. The Department of Justice report on the Michael Brown shooting found that Darren Wilson's account was corroborated by physical evidence and that there was no credible evidence that he willfully shot Brown as Brown was attempting to surrender or was otherwise not posing a threat. The merits of the report on the shooting death of Michael Brown are beyond the scope of this publication. Brown's death was, regardless of the law, yet another tragedy which scarred relationships between law enforcement and African-American communities.

I. REPORT SUMMARY

THE CIVIL RIGHTS DIVISION OF THE UNITED STATES DEPARTMENT OF Justice opened its investigation of the Ferguson Police Department ("FPD") on September 4, 2014. This investigation was initiated under the pattern-or-practice provision of the Violent Crime Control and Law Enforcement Act of 1994, 42 U.S.C. § 14141, the Omnibus Crime Control and Safe Streets Act of 1968, 42 U.S.C. § 3789d ("Safe Streets Act"), and Title VI of the Civil Rights Act of 1964, 42 U.S.C. § 2000d ("Title VI"). This investigation has revealed a pattern or practice of unlawful conduct within the Ferguson Police Department that violates the First, Fourth, and Fourteenth Amendments to the United States Constitution, and federal statutory law.

Over the course of the investigation, we interviewed City officials, including City Manager John Shaw, Mayor James Knowles, Chief of Police Thomas Jackson, Municipal Judge Ronald Brockmeyer, the Municipal Court Clerk, Ferguson's Finance Director, half of FPD's sworn officers, and others. We spent, collectively, approximately 100 person-days onsite in Ferguson. We participated in ride-alongs with on-duty officers, reviewed over 35,000 pages of police records as well as thousands of emails and other electronic materials provided by the police department. Enlisting the assistance of statistical experts, we analyzed FPD's data on stops, searches, citations, and arrests, as well as data collected by the municipal court. We observed four separate sessions of Ferguson Municipal Court, interviewing dozens of people charged with local offenses, and we reviewed third-party studies regarding municipal court practices in Ferguson and St. Louis County more broadly. As in all of our investigations, we sought to engage

1

the local community, conducting hundreds of in-person and telephone interviews of individuals who reside in Ferguson or who have had interactions with the police department. We contacted ten neighborhood associations and met with each group that responded to us, as well as several other community groups and advocacy organizations. Throughout the investigation, we relied on two police chiefs who accompanied us to Ferguson and who themselves interviewed City and police officials, spoke with community members, and reviewed FPD policies and incident reports.

We thank the City officials and the rank-and-file officers who have cooperated with this investigation and provided us with insights into the operation of the police department, including the municipal court. Notwithstanding our findings about Ferguson's approach to law enforcement and the policing culture it creates, we found many Ferguson police officers and other City employees to be dedicated public servants striving each day to perform their duties lawfully and with respect for all members of the Ferguson community. The importance of their often-selfless work cannot be overstated.

We are also grateful to the many members of the Ferguson community who have met with us to share their experiences. It became clear during our many conversations with Ferguson residents from throughout the City that many residents, black and white, genuinely embrace Ferguson's diversity and want to reemerge from the events of recent months a truly inclusive, united community. This Report is intended to strengthen those efforts by recognizing the harms caused by Ferguson's law enforcement practices so that those harms can be better understood and overcome.

Ferguson's law enforcement practices are shaped by the City's focus on revenue rather than by public safety needs. This emphasis on revenue has compromised the institutional character of Ferguson's police department, contributing to a pattern of unconstitutional policing, and has also shaped its municipal court, leading to procedures that raise due process concerns and inflict unnecessary harm on members of the Ferguson community. Further, Ferguson's police and municipal court practices both reflect and exacerbate existing racial bias, including racial stereotypes. Ferguson's own data establish clear racial disparities that adversely impact African Americans. The evidence shows that discriminatory intent is part of the reason for these disparities. Over time, Ferguson's police and municipal court practices have sown deep mistrust between parts of the community and the police department, undermining law enforcement legitimacy among African Americans in particular.

Focus on Generating Revenue

The City budgets for sizeable increases in municipal fines and fees each year, exhorts police and court staff to deliver those revenue increases, and closely monitors whether those increases are achieved. City officials routinely urge Chief Jackson to generate more revenue through enforcement. In March 2010, for instance, the City Finance Director wrote to Chief Jackson that "unless ticket writing ramps up significantly before the end of the year, it will be hard to significantly raise collections next year. . . . Given that we are looking at a substantial sales tax shortfall, it's not an insignificant issue." Similarly, in March 2013, the Finance Director wrote to the City Manager: "Court fees are anticipated to rise about 7.5%. I did ask the Chief if he thought the PD could deliver 10% increase. He indicated they could try." The importance of focusing on revenue generation is communicated to FPD officers. Ferguson police officers from all ranks told us that revenue generation is stressed heavily within the police department, and that the message comes from City leadership. The evidence we reviewed supports this perception.

Police Practices

The City's emphasis on revenue generation has a profound effect on FPD's approach to law enforcement. Patrol assignments and schedules are geared toward aggressive enforcement of Ferguson's municipal code, with insufficient thought given to whether enforcement strategies promote public safety or unnecessarily undermine community trust and cooperation.

Officer evaluations and promotions depend to an inordinate degree on "productivity," meaning the number of citations issued. Partly as a consequence of City and FPD priorities, many officers appear to see some residents, especially those who live in Ferguson's predominantly African-American neighborhoods, less as constituents to be protected than as potential offenders and sources of revenue.

This culture within FPD influences officer activities in all areas of policing, beyond just ticketing. Officers expect and demand compliance even when they lack legal authority. They are inclined to interpret the exercise of free-speech rights as unlawful disobedience, innocent movements as physical threats, indications of mental or physical illness as belligerence. Police supervisors and leadership do too little to ensure that officers act in accordance with law and policy, and rarely respond meaningfully to civilian complaints of officer misconduct. The result is a pattern of stops without reasonable suspicion and arrests without probable cause in violation of the Fourth Amendment; infringement on free expression, as well as retaliation for protected expression, in violation of the First Amendment; and excessive force in violation of the Fourth Amendment.

Even relatively routine misconduct by Ferguson police officers can have significant consequences for the people whose rights are violated. For example, in the summer of 2012, a 32-year-old African-American man sat in his car cooling off after playing basketball in a Ferguson public park. An officer pulled up behind the man's car, blocking him in, and demanded the man's Social Security number and identification. Without any cause, the officer accused the man of being a pedophile, referring to the presence of children in the park, and ordered the man out of his car for a pat-down, although the officer had no reason to believe the man was armed. The officer also asked to search the man's car. The man objected, citing his constitutional rights. In response, the officer arrested the man, reportedly at gunpoint, charging him with eight violations of Ferguson's municipal code. One charge, Making a False Declaration, was for initially providing the short form of his first name (e.g., "Mike" instead of "Michael"), and an address which, although legitimate, was different from the one on his driver's license. Another charge was for not wearing a seat belt, even though he was seated in a parked car. The officer also charged the man both with having an expired operator's license, and with having no operator's license in his possession. The man told us that, because of these charges, he lost his job as a contractor with the federal government that he had held for years.

Municipal Court Practices

Ferguson has allowed its focus on revenue generation to fundamentally compromise the role of Ferguson's municipal court. The municipal court does not act as a neutral arbiter of the law or a check on unlawful police conduct. Instead, the court primarily uses its judicial authority as the means to compel the payment of fines and fees that advance the City's financial interests. This has led to court practices that violate the Fourteenth Amendment's due process and equal protection requirements. The court's practices also impose unnecessary harm, overwhelmingly on African-American individuals, and run counter to public safety.

Most strikingly, the court issues municipal arrest warrants not on the basis of public safety needs, but rather as a routine response to missed court appearances and required fine payments. In 2013 alone, the court issued over 9,000 warrants on cases stemming in large part from minor violations such as parking infractions, traffic tickets, or housing code violations. Jail time would be considered far too harsh a penalty for the great majority of these code violations, yet Ferguson's municipal court routinely issues warrants for people to be arrested and incarcerated for failing to timely pay related fines and fees. Under state law, a failure to appear in municipal court on a traffic charge involving a moving violation also results in a license suspension. Ferguson has made this penalty even more onerous by only allowing the suspension to be lifted after payment of an owed fine is made in full. Further, until recently, Ferguson also added charges, fines, and fees for each missed appearance and payment. Many pending cases still include such charges that were imposed before the court recently eliminated them, making it as difficult as before for people to resolve these cases.

The court imposes these severe penalties for missed appearances and payments even as several of the court's practices create unnecessary barriers to resolving a municipal violation. The court often fails to provide clear and accurate information regarding a person's charges or court obligations. And the court's fine assessment procedures do not adequately provide for a defendant to seek a fine reduction on account of financial incapacity or to seek alternatives to payment such as community service. City and court officials have adhered to these court practices despite acknowledging their needlessly harmful consequences. In August 2013, for example, one City Councilmember wrote to the City Manager, the Mayor, and other City officials lamenting the lack of a community service option and noted the benefits of such a program, including that it would "keep those people that simply don't have the money to pay their fines from constantly being arrested and going to jail, only to be released and do it all over again."

Together, these court practices exacerbate the harm of Ferguson's unconstitutional police practices. They impose a particular hardship upon Ferguson's most vulnerable residents, especially upon those living in or near poverty. Minor offenses can generate crippling debts, result in jail time because of an inability to pay, and result in the loss of a driver's license, employment, or housing.

We spoke, for example, with an African-American woman who has a still-pending case stemming from 2007, when, on a single occasion, she parked her car illegally. She received two citations and a $151 fine, plus fees. The woman, who experienced financial difficulties and periods of homelessness over several years, was charged with seven Failure to Appear offenses for missing court dates or fine payments on her parking tickets between 2007 and 2010. For each Failure to Appear, the court issued an arrest warrant and imposed new fines and fees. From 2007 to 2014, the woman was arrested twice, spent six days in jail, and paid $550 to the court for the events stemming from this single instance of illegal parking. Court records show that she twice attempted to make partial payments of $25 and $50, but the court returned those payments, refusing to accept anything less than payment in full. One of those payments was later accepted, but only after the court's letter rejecting payment by money order was returned as undeliverable. This woman is now making regular payments on the fine. As of December 2014, over seven years later, despite initially owing a $151 fine and having already paid $550, she still owed $541.

Racial Bias

Ferguson's approach to law enforcement both reflects and reinforces racial bias, including stereotyping. The harms of Ferguson's police and court practices are borne disproportionately by African Americans, and there is evidence that this is due in part to intentional discrimination on the basis of race.

Ferguson's law enforcement practices overwhelmingly impact African Americans. Data collected by the Ferguson Police Department from 2012 to 2014 shows that African Americans account for 85% of vehicle stops, 90% of citations, and 93% of arrests made by FPD officers, despite comprising only 67% of Ferguson's population. African Americans are more than twice as likely as white drivers to be searched during vehicle stops even after controlling for non-race based variables such as the reason the vehicle stop was initiated, but are found in possession of contraband 26% less often than white drivers, suggesting officers are impermissibly considering race as a factor when determining whether to search. African Americans are more likely to be cited and arrested following a stop regardless of why the stop was initiated and are more likely to receive multiple citations during a single incident. From 2012 to 2014, FPD issued four or more citations to African Americans on 73 occasions, but issued four or more citations to non-African Americans only twice. FPD appears to bring certain offenses almost exclusively against African Americans. For example, from 2011 to 2013, African Americans accounted for 95% of Manner of Walking in Roadway charges, and 94% of all Failure to Comply charges. Notably, with respect to speeding charges brought by FPD, the evidence shows not only that African Americans are represented at disproportionately high rates overall, but also that the disparate impact of FPD's enforcement practices on African Americans is 48% larger when citations are issued not on the basis of radar or laser, but by some other method, such as the officer's own visual assessment.

These disparities are also present in FPD's use of force. Nearly 90% of documented force used by FPD officers was used against African Americans. In every canine bite incident for which racial information is available, the person bitten was African American.

Municipal court practices likewise cause disproportionate harm to African Americans. African Americans are 68% less likely than others to have their cases dismissed by the court, and are more likely to have their cases last longer and result in more required court encounters. African Americans are at least 50% more likely to have their cases lead to an arrest warrant, and accounted for 92% of cases in which an arrest warrant was issued by the Ferguson Municipal Court in 2013. Available data show that, of those actually arrested by FPD only because of an outstanding municipal warrant, 96% are African American.

Our investigation indicates that this disproportionate burden on African Americans cannot be explained by any difference in the rate at which people of different races violate the law. Rather, our investigation has revealed that these disparities occur, at least in part, because of unlawful bias against and stereotypes about African Americans. We have found substantial evidence of racial bias among police and court staff in Ferguson. For example, we discovered emails circulated by police supervisors and court staff that stereotype racial minorities as criminals, including one email that joked about an abortion by an African-American woman being a means of crime control.

City officials have frequently asserted that the harsh and disparate results of Ferguson's law enforcement system do not indicate problems with police or court practices, but instead reflect a pervasive lack of "personal responsibility" among "certain segments" of the community. Our investigation has found that the practices about which area residents have complained are in fact unconstitutional and unduly harsh. But the City's personal-responsibility refrain is telling: it reflects many of the same racial stereotypes found in the emails between police and court supervisors. This evidence of bias and stereotyping, together with evidence that Ferguson has long recognized but failed to correct the consistent racial disparities caused by its police and court practices, demonstrates that the discriminatory effects of Ferguson's conduct are driven at least in part by discriminatory intent in violation of the Fourteenth Amendment.

Community Distrust

Since the August 2014 shooting death of Michael Brown, the lack of trust between the Ferguson Police Department and a significant portion of Ferguson's residents, especially African Americans, has become undeniable. The causes of this distrust and division, however, have been the subject of debate. Police and other City officials, as well as some Ferguson residents, have insisted to us that the public outcry is attributable to "outside agitators" who do not reflect the opinions of "real Ferguson residents." That view is at odds with the facts we have gathered during our investigation. Our investigation has shown that distrust of the Ferguson Police Department is longstanding and largely attributable to Ferguson's approach to law enforcement. This approach results in patterns of unnecessarily aggressive and at times unlawful policing; reinforces the harm of discriminatory stereotypes; discourages a culture of accountability; and neglects community engagement. In recent years, FPD has moved away from the modest community policing efforts it previously had implemented, reducing opportunities for positive police-community interactions, and losing the little familiarity it had with some African-American neighborhoods. The confluence of policing to raise revenue and racial bias thus has resulted in practices that not only violate the Constitution and cause direct harm to the individuals whose rights are violated, but also undermine community trust, especially among many African Americans. As a consequence of these practices, law enforcement is seen as illegitimate, and the partnerships necessary for public safety are, in some areas, entirely absent.

Restoring trust in law enforcement will require recognition of the harms caused by Ferguson's law enforcement practices, and diligent, committed collaboration with the entire Ferguson community. At the conclusion of this report, we have broadly identified the changes that are necessary for meaningful and sustainable reform. These measures build upon a number of other recommended changes we communicated verbally to the Mayor, Police Chief, and City Manager in September so that Ferguson could begin immediately to address problems as we identified them. As a result of those recommendations, the City and police department have already begun to make some changes to municipal court and police practices. We commend City officials for beginning to take steps to address some of the concerns we have already raised. Nonetheless, these changes are only a small part of the reform necessary. Addressing the deeply embedded constitutional deficiencies we found demands an entire reorientation of law enforcement in Ferguson. The City must replace revenue-driven policing with a system grounded in the principles of community policing and police legitimacy, in which people are equally protected and treated with compassion, regardless of race.

II. BACKGROUND

THE CITY OF FERGUSON IS ONE OF 89 MUNICIPALITIES IN ST. LOUIS County, Missouri.[1]

According to United States Census Data from 2010, Ferguson is home to roughly 21,000 residents.[2] While Ferguson's total population has stayed relatively constant in recent decades, Ferguson's racial demographics have changed dramatically during that time. In 1990, 74% of Ferguson's population was white, while 25% was black.[3] By 2000, African Americans became the new majority, making up 52% of the City's population.[4] According to the 2010 Census, the black population in Ferguson has grown to 67%, whereas the white population has decreased to 29%.[5] According to the 2009–2013 American Community Survey, 25% of the City's population lives below the federal poverty level.[6]

Residents of Ferguson elect a Mayor and six individuals to serve on a City Council. The City Council appoints a City Manager to an indefinite term, subject to removal by a Council vote. *See* Ferguson City Charter § 4.1. The City Manager serves as chief executive and administrative officer of the City of Ferguson, and is responsible for all affairs of the City. The City Manager directs and supervises all City departments, including the Ferguson Police Department.

The current Chief of Police, Thomas Jackson, has commanded the police department since he was appointed by the City Manager in 2010. The department has a total of 54 sworn officers divided among several divisions. The patrol division is the largest division; 28 patrol officers are supervised by four sergeants, two lieutenants, and a captain. Each of the four

11

patrol squads has a canine officer. While all patrol officers engage in traffic enforcement, FPD also has a dedicated traffic officer responsible for collecting traffic stop data required by the state of Missouri. FPD has two School Resource Officers ("SROs"), one who is assigned to the McCluer South-Berkeley High School and one who is assigned to the Ferguson Middle School. FPD has a single officer assigned to be the "Community Resource Officer," who attends community meetings, serves as FPD's public relations liaison, and is charged with collecting crime data. FPD operates its own jail, which has ten individual cells and a large holding cell. The jail is staffed by three non-sworn correctional officers. Of the 54 sworn officers currently serving in FPD, four are African American.

FPD officers are authorized to initiate charges—by issuing citations or summonses, or by making arrests—under both the municipal code and state law. Ferguson's municipal code addresses nearly every aspect of civic life for those who live in Ferguson, and regulates the conduct of all who work, travel through, or otherwise visit the City. In addition to mirroring some non-felony state law violations, such as assault, stealing, and traffic violations, the code establishes housing violations, such as High Grass and Weeds; requirements for permits to rent an apartment or use the City's trash service; animal control ordinances, such as Barking Dog and Dog Running at Large; and a number of other violations, such as Manner of Walking in Roadway. *See, e.g.*, Ferguson Mun. Code §§ 29-16 *et seq.*; 37-1 *et seq.*; 46-27; 6-5, 6-11; 44344.

FPD files most charges as municipal offenses, not state violations, even when an analogous state offense exists. Between July 1, 2010, and June 30, 2014, the City of Ferguson issued approximately 90,000 citations and summonses for municipal violations. Notably, the City issued nearly 50% more citations in the last year of that time period than it did in the first. This increase in enforcement has not been driven by a rise in serious crime. While the ticketing rate has increased dramatically, the number of charges for many of the most serious offenses covered by the municipal code—e.g., Assault, Driving While Intoxicated, and Stealing—has remained relatively constant.[7]

Because the overwhelming majority of FPD's enforcement actions are brought under the municipal code, most charges are processed and resolved by the Ferguson Municipal Court, which has primary jurisdiction over all code violations. Ferguson Mun. Code § 13-2. Ferguson's municipal court operates as part of the police department. The court is supervised by the Ferguson Chief of Police, is considered part of the police department for City organizational purposes, and is physically located within the police station. Court staff report directly to the Chief of Police. Thus, if the City Manager or other City officials issue a court-related directive, it is typically sent to the Police Chief's attention. In recent weeks, City officials informed us that they are considering plans to bring the court under the supervision of the City Finance Director.

A Municipal Judge presides over court sessions. The Municipal Judge is not hired or supervised by the Chief of Police, but is instead nominated by the City Manager and elected by the City Council. The Judge serves a two-year term, subject to reappointment. The current Municipal Judge, Ronald Brockmeyer, has presided in Ferguson for approximately ten years. The City's Prosecuting Attorney and her assistants officially prosecute all actions before the court, although in practice most cases are resolved without trial or a prosecutor's involvement. The current Prosecuting Attorney was appointed in April 2011. At the time of her appointment, the Prosecuting Attorney was already serving as City Attorney, and she continues to serve in that separate capacity, which entails providing general counsel and representation to the City. The Municipal Judge, Court Clerk, Prosecuting Attorney, and all assistant court clerks are white.

While the Municipal Judge presides over court sessions, the Court Clerk, who is employed under the Police Chief's supervision, plays the most significant role in managing the court and exercises broad discretion in conducting the court's daily operations. Ferguson's municipal code confers broad authority on the Court Clerk, including the authority to collect all fines and fees, accept guilty pleas, sign and issue subpoenas, and approve bond determinations. Ferguson Mun. Code § 13-7. Indeed, the Court Clerk and assistant clerks routinely perform duties that are, for all practical purposes, judicial. For example, documents indicate that court clerks have disposed of charges without the Municipal Judge's involvement.

The court officially operates subject to the oversight of the presiding judge of the St. Louis County Circuit Court (21st Judicial Circuit) under the rules promulgated by that Circuit Court and the Missouri Supreme Court. Notwithstanding these rules, the City of Ferguson and the court itself retain considerable power to establish and amend court practices and procedures. The Ferguson municipal code sets forth a limited number of protocols that the court must follow, but the code leaves most aspects of court operations to the discretion of the court itself. *See* Ferguson Mun. Code Ch. 13, Art. III. The code also explicitly authorizes the Municipal Judge to "make and adopt such rules of practice and procedure as are necessary to hear and decide matters pending before the municipal court." Ferguson Mun. Code § 13-29.

The Ferguson Municipal Court has the authority to issue and enforce judgments, issue warrants for search and arrest, hold parties in contempt, and order imprisonment as a *penalty* for contempt. The court may conduct trials, although it does so rarely, and most charges are resolved without one. Upon resolution of a charge, the court has the authority to impose fines, fees, and imprisonment when violations are found. Specifically, the court can impose imprisonment in the Ferguson City Jail for up to three months, a fine of up to $1,000, or a combination thereof. It is rare for the court to sentence anyone to jail as a penalty for a violation of the municipal code; indeed, the Municipal Judge reports that he has done so only once. Rather, the court almost always imposes a monetary penalty payable to the City of Ferguson, plus court fees. Nonetheless, as discussed in detail below, the court issues arrest warrants when a person misses a court appearance or fails to timely pay a fine. As a result, violations that would normally not result in a penalty of imprisonment can, and frequently do, lead to municipal warrants, arrests, and jail time.

As the number of charges initiated by FPD has increased in recent years, the size of the court's docket has also increased. According to data the City reported to the Missouri State Courts Administrator, at the end of fiscal year 2009, the municipal court had roughly 24,000 traffic cases and 28,000 non-traffic cases pending. As of October 31, 2014, both of those figures had roughly doubled to 53,000 and 50,000 cases, respectively. In fiscal year 2009, 16,178 new cases were filed, and 8,727 were resolved. In 2014, by contrast, 24,256 new offenses were filed, and 10,975 offenses were resolved. The court holds three or four sessions per month, and each session lasts no more than three hours. It is not uncommon for as many as 500 people to appear before the court in a single session, exceeding the court's physical capacity and leading individuals to line up outside of court waiting to be heard. Many people have multiple offenses pending; accordingly, the court typically considers 1,200–1,500 offenses in a single session, and has in the past considered over 2,000 offenses during one sitting. Previously there was a cap on the number of offenses that could be assigned to a particular docket date. Given that cap, and the significant increase in municipal citations in recent years, a problem developed in December 2011 in which more citations were issued than court sessions could timely accommodate. At one point court dates were initially scheduled as far as six months after the date of the citation. To address this problem, court staff first raised the cap to allow 1,000 offenses to be assigned to a single court date and later eliminated the cap altogether. To handle the increasing caseload, the City Manager also requested and secured City Council approval to fund additional court positions, noting in January 2013 that "each month we are setting new all-time records in fines and forfeitures," that this was overburdening court staff, and that the funding for the additional positions "will be more than covered by the increase in revenues."

III. FERGUSON LAW ENFORCEMENT EFFORTS ARE FOCUSED ON GENERATING REVENUE

CITY OFFICIALS HAVE CONSISTENTLY SET MAXIMIZING REVENUE AS the priority for Ferguson's law enforcement activity. Ferguson generates a significant and increasing amount of revenue from the enforcement of code provisions. The City has budgeted for, and achieved, significant increases in revenue from municipal code enforcement over the last several years, and these increases are projected to continue. Of the $11.07 million in general fund revenue the City collected in fiscal year 2010, $1.38 million came from fines and fees collected by the court; similarly, in fiscal year 2011, the City's general fund revenue of $11.44 million included $1.41 million from fines and fees. In its budget for fiscal year 2012, however, the City predicted that revenue from municipal fines and fees would increase over 30% from the previous year's amount to $1.92 million; the court exceeded that target, collecting $2.11 million. In its budget for fiscal year 2013, the City budgeted for fines and fees to yield $2.11 million; the court exceeded that target as well, collecting $2.46 million. For 2014, the City budgeted for the municipal court to generate $2.63 million in revenue. The City has not yet made public the actual revenue collected that year, although budget documents forecasted lower revenue than was budgeted. Nonetheless, for fiscal year 2015, the City's budget anticipates fine and fee revenues to account for $3.09 million of a projected $13.26 million in general fund revenues.[8]

City, police, and court officials for years have worked in concert to maximize revenue at every stage of the enforcement process, beginning with how fines and fine enforcement processes are established. In a February

2011 report requested by the City Council at a Financial Planning Session and drafted by Ferguson's Finance Director with contributions from Chief Jackson, the Finance Director reported on "efforts to increase efficiencies and maximize collection" by the municipal court. The report included an extensive comparison of Ferguson's fines to those of surrounding municipalities and noted with approval that Ferguson's fines are "at or near the top of the list." The chart noted, for example, that while other municipalities' parking fines generally range from $5 to $100, Ferguson's is $102. The chart noted also that the charge for "Weeds/Tall Grass" was as little as $5 in one city but, in Ferguson, it ranged from $77 to $102. The report stated that the acting prosecutor had reviewed the City's "high volume offenses" and "started recommending higher fines on these cases, and recommending probation only infrequently." While the report stated that this recommendation was because of a "large volume of non-compliance," the recommendation was in fact emphasized as one of several ways that the code enforcement system had been honed to produce more revenue.

In combination with a high fine schedule, the City directs FPD to aggressively enforce the municipal code. City and police leadership pressure officers to write citations, independent of any public safety need, and rely on citation productivity to fund the City budget. In an email from March 2010, the Finance Director wrote to Chief Jackson that "unless ticket writing ramps up significantly before the end of the year, it will be hard to significantly raise collections next year. What are your thoughts? Given that we are looking at a substantial sales tax shortfall, it's not an insignificant issue." Chief Jackson responded that the City would see an increase in fines once more officers were hired and that he could target the $1.5 million forecast. Significantly, Chief Jackson stated that he was also "looking at different shift schedules which will place more officers on the street, which in turn will increase traffic enforcement per shift." Shortly thereafter, FPD switched to the 12-hour shift schedule for its patrol officers, which FPD continues to use. Law enforcement experience has shown that this schedule makes community policing more difficult—a concern that we have also heard directly from FPD officers. Nonetheless, while FPD heavily considered the revenue implications of the 12-hour shift and certain other factors such as its impact on overtime and sick time usage, we have found no evidence that FPD considered the consequences for positive community engagement. The City's 2014 budget itself stated that since December 2010, "the percent of [FPD] resources allocated to traffic enforcement has increased," and "[a]s a result, traffic enforcement related collections increased" in the following two years. The 2015 budget added that even after those initial increases, in fiscal year 2012–2013, FPD was once again "successful in increasing their proportion of resources dedicated to traffic enforcement" and increasing collections.

As directed, FPD supervisors and line officers have undertaken the aggressive code enforcement required to meet the City's revenue generation expectations. As discussed below in Part III.A., FPD officers routinely conduct stops that have little relation to public safety and a questionable basis in law. FPD officers routinely issue multiple citations during a single stop, often for the same violation. Issuing three or four charges in one stop is not uncommon in Ferguson. Officers sometimes write six, eight, or, in at least one instance, fourteen citations for a single encounter. Indeed, officers told us that some compete to see who can issue the largest number of citations during a single stop.

The February 2011 report to the City Council notes that the acting prosecutor—with the apparent approval of the Police Chief—"talked with police officers about ensuring all necessary summonses are written for each incident, i.e. when DWI charges are issued, are the correct companion charges being issued, such as speeding, failure to maintain a single lane, no insurance, and no seat belt, etc." The prosecutor noted that "[t]his is done to ensure that a proper resolution to all cases is being achieved and that the court is maintaining the correct volume for offenses occurring within the city." Notably, the "correct volume" of law enforcement is uniformly presented in City documents as related to revenue generation, rather than in terms of what is necessary to promote public safety.[9] Each month, the municipal court provides FPD supervisors with a list of the number of tickets issued by each officer and each squad. Supervisors have posted the list inside the police station, a tactic officers say is meant to push them to write more citations.

The Captain of FPD's Patrol Division regularly communicates with his Division commanders regarding the need to increase traffic "productivity," and productivity is a common topic at squad meetings. Patrol Division supervisors monitor productivity through monthly "self-initiated activity reports" and instruct officers to increase production when those reports show they have not issued enough citations. In April 2010, for example, a patrol supervisor criticized a sergeant for his squad only issuing 25 tickets in a month, including one officer who issued "a grand total" of 11 tickets to six people on three days "devoted to traffic stops." In November 2011, the same patrol supervisor wrote to his patrol lieutenants and sergeants that "[t]he monthly self-initiated activity totals just came out," and they "may want to advise [their] officers who may be interested in the open detective position that one of the categories to be considered when deciding on the eligibility list will be self-initiated activity." The supervisor continued: "Have any of you heard comments such as, why should I produce when I know I'm not getting a raise? Well, some people are about to find out why." The email concludes with the instruction to "[k]eep in mind, productivity (self-initiated activity) cannot decline for next year."

FPD has communicated to officers not only that they must focus on bringing in revenue, but that the department has little concern with how officers do this. FPD's weak systems of supervision, review, and accountability, discussed below in Part III.A., have sent a potent message to officers that their violations of law and policy will be tolerated, provided that officers continue to be "productive" in making arrests and writing citations. Where officers fail to meet productivity goals, supervisors have been instructed to alter officer assignments or impose discipline. In August 2012, the Captain of the Patrol Division instructed other patrol supervisors that, "[f]or those officers who are not keeping up an acceptable level of productivity and they have already been addressed at least once if not multiple times, take it to the next level." He continued: "As we have discussed already, regardless of the seniority and experience take the officer out of the cover car position and assign them to prisoner pick up and bank runs. . . . Failure to perform *can* result in disciplinary action not just a bad evaluation." Performance evaluations also heavily emphasize productivity. A June 2013 evaluation indicates one of the "Performance-Related Areas of Improvements" as "Increase/consistent in productivity, the ability to maintain an average ticket [sic] of 28 per month."

Not all officers within FPD agree with this approach. Several officers commented on the futility of imposing mounting penalties on people who will never be able to afford them. One member of FPD's command staff quoted an old adage, asking: "How can you get blood from a turnip?" Another questioned why FPD did not allow residents to use their limited resources to fix equipment violations, such as broken headlights, rather than paying that money to the City, as fixing the equipment violation would more directly benefit public safety.[10]

However, enough officers—at all ranks—have internalized this message that a culture of reflexive enforcement action, unconcerned with whether the police action actually promotes public safety, and unconcerned with the impact the decision has on individual lives or community trust as a whole, has taken hold within FPD. One commander told us, for example, that when he admonished an officer for writing too many tickets, the officer challenged the commander, asking if the commander was telling him not to do his job. When another commander tried to discipline an officer for over-ticketing, he got the same response from the Chief of Police: "No discipline for doing your job."

The City closely monitors whether FPD's enforcement efforts are bringing in revenue at the desired rate. Consistently over the last several years, the Police Chief has directly reported to City officials FPD's successful efforts at raising revenue through policing, and City officials have continued to encourage those efforts and request regular updates. For example, in June 2010, at the request of the City, the Chief prepared a report comparing court revenues in Ferguson to court revenues for cities of similar sizes. The Chief's email sending the report to the City Manager notes that, "of the 80 St. Louis County Municipal Courts reporting revenue, only 8, including Ferguson, have collections greater than one million dollars." In the February 2011 report referenced above, Chief Jackson discussed various obstacles to officers writing tickets in previous months, such as training, injury leave, and officer deployment to Iraq, but noted that those factors had subsided and that, as a result, revenues were increasing. The acting prosecutor echoed these statements, stating "we now have several new officers writing tickets, and as a result our overall ticket volume is increasing by 400–700 tickets per month. This increased volume will lead to larger dockets this year and should have a direct effect in increasing overall revenue to the municipal court."

Similarly, in March 2011, the Chief reported to the City Manager that court revenue in February was $179,862.50, and that the total "beat our next biggest month in the last four years by over $17,000," to which the City Manager responded: "Wonderful!" In a June 2011 email from Chief Jackson to the Finance Director and City Manager, the Chief reported that "May is the 6th straight month in which court revenue (gross) has exceeded the previous year." The City Manager again applauded the Chief's efforts, and the Finance Director added praise, noting that the Chief is "substantially in control of the outcome." The Finance Director further recommended in this email greater police and judicial enforcement to "have a profound effect on collections." Similarly, in a January 2013 email from Chief Jackson to the City Manager, the Chief reported: "Municipal Court gross revenue for calendar year 2012 passed the $2,000,000 mark for the first time in history, reaching $2,066,050 (not including red light photo enforcement)." The City Manager responded: "Awesome! Thanks!" In one March 2012 email, the Captain of the Patrol Division reported directly to the City Manager that court collections in February 2012 reached $235,000, and that this was the first month collections ever exceeded $200,000. The Captain noted that "[t]he [court clerk] girls have been swamped all day with a line of people paying off fines today. Since 9:30 this morning there hasn't been less than 5 people waiting in line and for the last three hours 10 to 15 people at all times." The City Manager enthusiastically reported the Captain's email to the City Council and congratulated both police department and court staff on their "great work."

Even as officers have answered the call for greater revenue through code enforcement, the City continues to urge the police department to bring in more money. In a March 2013 email, the Finance Director wrote: "Court fees are anticipated to rise about 7.5%. I did ask the Chief if he thought the PD could deliver 10% increase. He indicated they could try." Even more recently, the City's Finance Director stated publicly that Ferguson intends to make up a 2014 revenue shortfall in 2015 through municipal code enforcement, stating to Bloomberg News that "[t]here's about a million-dollar increase in public-safety fines to make up the difference."[11] The City issued a statement to "refute[]" the Bloomberg article in part because it "insinuates" an "over reliance on municipal court fines as a primary source of revenues when in fact they represented less than 12% of city revenues for the last fiscal year." But there is no dispute that the City budget does, in fact, forecast an increase of nearly a million dollars in municipal code enforcement fines and fees in 2015 as reported in the Bloomberg News report.

The City goes so far as to direct FPD to develop enforcement strategies and initiatives, not to better protect the public, but to raise more revenue. In an April 2014 communication from the Finance Director to Chief Jackson and the City Manager, the Finance Director recommended immediate implementation of an "I-270 traffic enforcement initiative" in order to "begin to fill the revenue pipeline." The Finance Director's email attached a computation of the net revenues that would be generated by the initiative, which required paying five officers overtime for highway traffic enforcement for a four-hour shift. The Finance Director stated that "there is nothing to keep us from running this initiative 1, 2, 3, 4, 5, 6, or even 7 days a week. Admittedly at 7 days per week[] we would see diminishing returns." Indeed, in a separate email to FPD supervisors, the Patrol Captain explained that "[t]he plan behind this [initiative] is to PRODUCE traffic tickets, not provide easy OT." There is no indication that anyone considered whether community policing and public safety would be better served by devoting five overtime officers to neighborhood policing instead of a "revenue pipeline" of highway traffic enforcement. Rather, the only downsides to the program that City officials appear to have considered are that "this initiative requires

60 to 90 [days] of lead time to turn citations into cash," and that Missouri law caps the proportion of revenue that can come from municipal fines at 30%, which limits the extent to which the program can be used. *See* Mo. Rev. Stat. § 302.341.2. With regard to the statewide-cap issue, the Finance Director advised: "As the RLCs [Red Light Cameras] net revenues ramp up to whatever we believe its annualized rate will be, then we can figure out how to balance the two programs to get their total revenues as close as possible to the statutory limit of 30%."[12]

The City has made clear to the Police Chief and the Municipal Judge that revenue generation must also be a priority in court operations. The Finance Director's February 2011 report to the City Council notes that "Judge Brockmeyer was first appointed in 2003, and during this time has been successful in significantly increasing court collections over the years." The report includes a list of "what he has done to help in the areas of court efficiency and revenue." The list, drafted by Judge Brockmeyer, approvingly highlights the creation of additional fees, many of which are widely considered abusive and may be unlawful, including several that the City has repealed during the pendency of our investigation. These include a $50 fee charged each time a person has a pending municipal arrest warrant cleared, and a "failure to appear fine," which the Judge noted is "increased each time the Defendant fails to appear in court or pay a fine." The Judge also noted increasing fines for repeat offenders, "especially in regard to housing violations, [which] have increased substantially and will continue to be increased upon subsequent violations." The February 2011 report notes Judge Brockmeyer's statement that "none of these changes could have taken place without the cooperation of the Court Clerk, the Chief of Police, and the Prosecutor's Office." Indeed, the acting prosecutor noted in the report that "I have denied defendants' needless requests for continuance from the payment docket in an effort to aid in the court's efficient collection of its fines."

Court staff are keenly aware that the City considers revenue generation to be the municipal court's primary purpose. Revenue targets for court fines and fees are created in consultation not only with Chief Jackson, but also the Court Clerk. In one April 2010 exchange with Chief Jackson entitled "2011 Budget," for example, the Finance Director sought and received confirmation that the Police Chief and the Court Clerk would prepare targets for the court's fine and fee collections for subsequent years. Court staff take steps to ensure those targets are met in operating court. For example, in April 2011, the Court Clerk wrote to Judge Brockmeyer (copying Chief Jackson) that the fines the new Prosecuting Attorney was recommending were not high enough. The Clerk highlighted one case involving three Derelict Vehicle charges and a Failure to Comply charge that resulted in $76 in fines, and noted this "normally would have brought a fine of all three charges around $400." After describing another case that she believed warranted higher fines, the Clerk concluded: "We need to keep up our revenue." There is no indication that ability to pay or public safety goals were considered.

The City has been aware for years of concerns about the impact its focus on revenue has had on lawful police action and the fair administration of justice in Ferguson. It has disregarded those concerns—even concerns raised from within the City government—to avoid disturbing the court's ability to optimize revenue generation. In 2012, a Ferguson City Councilmember wrote to other City officials in opposition to Judge Brockmeyer's reappointment, stating that "[the Judge] does not listen to the testimony, does not review the reports or the criminal history of defendants, and doesn't let all the pertinent witnesses testify before rendering a verdict." The Councilmember then addressed the concern that "switching judges would/could lead to loss of revenue," arguing that even if such a switch did "lead to a slight loss, I think it's more important that cases are being handled properly and fairly." The City Manager acknowledged mixed reviews of the Judge's work but urged that the Judge be reappointed, noting that "[i]t goes without saying the City cannot afford to lose any efficiency in our Courts, nor experience any decrease in our Fines and Forfeitures."

IV. FERGUSON LAW ENFORCEMENT PRACTICES VIOLATE THE LAW AND UNDERMINE COMMUNITY TRUST, ESPECIALLY AMONG AFRICAN AMERICANS

FERGUSON'S STRATEGY OF REVENUE GENERATION THROUGH POLICing has fostered practices in the two central parts of Ferguson's law enforcement system—policing and the courts—that are themselves unconstitutional or that contribute to constitutional violations. In both parts of the system, these practices disproportionately harm African Americans. Further, the evidence indicates that this harm to African Americans stems, at least in part, from racial bias, including racial stereotyping. Ultimately, unlawful and harmful practices in policing and in the municipal court system erode police legitimacy and community trust, making policing in Ferguson less fair, less effective at promoting public safety, and less safe.

A. Ferguson's Police Practices

FPD's approach to law enforcement, shaped by the City's pressure to raise revenue, has resulted in a pattern and practice of constitutional violations. Officers violate the Fourth Amendment in stopping people without reasonable suspicion, arresting them without probable cause, and using unreasonable force. Officers frequently infringe on residents' First Amendment rights, interfering with their right to record police activities and making enforcement decisions based on the content of individuals' expression.

FPD's lack of systems to detect and hold officers responsible for misconduct reflects the department's focus on revenue generation at the expense of lawful policing and helps perpetuate the patterns of unconstitutional conduct we found. FPD fails to adequately supervise officers or review their enforcement actions. While FPD collects vehicle-stop data because it is required to do so by state law, it collects no reliable or consistent data regarding pedestrian stops, even though it has the technology to do so.[13] In Ferguson, officers will sometimes make an arrest without writing a report or even obtaining an incident number, and hundreds of reports can pile up for months without supervisors reviewing them. Officers' uses of force frequently go unreported, and are reviewed only laxly when reviewed at all. As a result of these deficient practices, stops, arrests, and uses of force that violate the law or FPD policy are rarely detected and often ignored when they are discovered.

1. FPD ENGAGES IN A PATTERN OF UNCONSTITUTIONAL STOPS AND ARRESTS IN VIOLATION OF THE FOURTH AMENDMENT

FPD's approach to law enforcement has led officers to conduct stops and arrests that violate the Constitution. We identified several elements to this pattern of misconduct. Frequently, officers stop people without reasonable suspicion or arrest them without probable cause. Officers rely heavily on the municipal "Failure to Comply" charge, which appears to be facially unconstitutional in part, and is frequently abused in practice. FPD also relies on a system of officer-generated arrest orders called "wanteds" that circumvents the warrant system and poses a significant risk of abuse. The data show, moreover, that FPD misconduct in the area of stops and arrests disproportionately impacts African Americans.

a. FPD Officers Frequently Detain People Without Reasonable Suspicion and Arrest People Without Probable Cause.

The Fourth Amendment protects individuals from unreasonable searches and seizures. Generally, a search or seizure is unreasonable "in the absence of individualized suspicion of wrongdoing." *City of Indianapolis v. Edmond*, 531 U.S. 32, 37 (2000). The Fourth Amendment permits law enforcement officers to briefly detain individuals for investigative purposes if the officers possess reasonable suspicion that criminal activity is afoot. *Terry v. Ohio*, 392 U.S. 1, 21 (1968). Reasonable suspicion exists when an "officer is aware of particularized, objective facts which, taken together with rational inferences from those facts, reasonably warrant suspicion that a crime is being committed." *United States v. Givens*, 763 F.3d 987, 989 (8th Cir. 2014) (internal quotation marks omitted). In addition, if the officer reasonably believes the person with whom he or she is dealing is armed and dangerous, the officer may conduct a protective search or frisk of the person's outer clothing. *United States v. Cotter*, 701 F.3d 544, 547 (8th Cir. 2012). Such a search is not justified on the basis of "inchoate and unparticularized suspicion;" rather, the "issue is whether a reasonably prudent man in the circumstances would be warranted in the belief that his safety or that of others was in danger." *Id.* (quoting *Terry*, 392 U.S. at 27). For an arrest to constitute a reasonable seizure under the Fourth Amendment, it must be supported by probable cause, which exists only if "the totality of facts based on reasonably trustworthy information would justify a prudent person in believing the individual arrested had committed an offense at the time of the arrest." *Stoner v. Watlingten*, 735 F.3d 799, 803 (8th Cir. 2013).

Under Missouri law, when making an arrest, "[t]he officer must inform the defendant by what authority he acts, and must also show the warrant if required." Mo. Rev. Stat. § 544.180. In reviewing FPD records, we found numerous incidents in which—based on the officer's own description of the detention—an officer detained an individual without articulable reasonable suspicion of criminal activity or arrested a person without probable cause. In none of these cases did the officer explain or justify his conduct.

For example, in July 2013 police encountered an African-American man in a parking lot while on their way to arrest someone else at an apartment building. Police knew that the encountered man was not the person they had come to arrest. Nonetheless, without even reasonable suspicion, they handcuffed the man, placed him in the back of a patrol car, and ran his record. It turned out he was the intended arrestee's landlord. The landlord went on to help the police enter the person's unit to effect the arrest, but he later filed a complaint alleging racial discrimination and unlawful detention. Ignoring the central fact that they had handcuffed a man and put him in a police car despite having no reason to believe he had done anything wrong, a sergeant vigorously defended FPD's actions, characterizing the detention as "minimal" and pointing out that the car was air conditioned. Even temporary detention, however, constitutes a deprivation of liberty and must be justified under the Fourth Amendment. *Whren v. United States*, 517 U.S. 806, 809–10 (1996).

Many of the unlawful stops we found appear to have been driven, in part, by an officer's desire to check whether the subject had a municipal arrest warrant pending. Several incidents suggest that officers are more concerned with issuing citations and generating charges than with addressing community needs. In October 2012, police officers pulled over an African-American man who had lived in Ferguson for 16 years, claiming that his passenger-side brake light was broken. The driver happened to have replaced the light recently and knew it to be functioning properly. Nonetheless, according to the man's written complaint, one officer stated, "let's see how many tickets you're going to get," while a second officer tapped his Electronic Control Weapon ("ECW") on the roof of the man's car. The officers wrote the man a citation for "tail light/reflector/license plate light out." They refused to let the man show them that his car's equipment was in order, warning him, "don't you get out of that car until you get to your house." The man, who believed he had been racially profiled, was so upset that he went to the police station that night to show a sergeant that his brakes and license plate light worked.

At times, the constitutional violations are even more blatant. An African-American man recounted to us an experience he had while sitting at a bus stop near Canfield Drive. According to the man, an FPD patrol car abruptly pulled up in front of him. The officer inside, a patrol lieutenant, rolled down his window and addressed the man:

Lieutenant: Get over here.
Bus Patron: Me?
Lieutenant: Get the f*** over here. Yeah, you.

Bus Patron: Why? What did I do?

Lieutenant: Give me your ID.

Bus Patron: Why?

Lieutenant: Stop being a smart ass and give me your ID.

The lieutenant ran the man's name for warrants. Finding none, he returned the ID and said, "get the hell out of my face." These allegations are consistent with other, independent allegations of misconduct that we heard about this particular lieutenant, and reflect the routinely disrespectful treatment many African Americans say they have come to expect from Ferguson police. That a lieutenant with supervisory responsibilities allegedly engaged in this conduct is further cause for concern.

This incident is also consistent with a pattern of suspicionless, legally unsupportable stops we found documented in FPD's records, described by FPD as "ped checks" or "pedestrian checks." Though at times officers use the term to refer to reasonable-suspicion-based pedestrian stops, or "*Terry* stops," they often use it when stopping a person with no objective, articulable suspicion. For example, one night in December 2013, officers went out and "ped. checked those wandering around" in Ferguson's apartment complexes. In another case, officers responded to a call about a man selling drugs by stopping a group of six African-American youths who, due to their numbers, did not match the facts of the call. The youths were "detained and ped checked." Officers invoke the term "ped check" as though it has some unique constitutional legitimacy. It does not. Officers may not detain a person, even briefly, without articulable reasonable suspicion. *Terry*, 392 U.S. at 21. To the extent that the words "ped check" suggest otherwise, the terminology alone is dangerous because it threatens to confuse officers' understanding of the law. Moreover, because FPD does not track or analyze pedestrian *Terry* stops—whether termed "ped checks" or something else—in any reliable way, they are especially susceptible to discriminatory or otherwise unlawful use.

As with its pattern of unconstitutional stops, FPD routinely makes arrests without probable cause. Frequently, officers arrest people for conduct that plainly does not meet the elements of the cited offense. For example, in November 2013, an officer approached five African-American young people listening to music in a car. Claiming to have smelled marijuana, the officer placed them under arrest for disorderly conduct based on their "gathering in a group for the purposes of committing illegal activity." The young people were detained and charged—some taken to jail, others delivered to their parents—despite the officer finding no marijuana, even after conducting an inventory search of the car. Similarly, in February 2012, an officer wrote an arrest notification ticket for Peace Disturbance for "loud music" coming from a car. The arrest ticket appears unlawful as the officer did not assert, and there is no other indication, that a third party was disturbed by the music—an element of the offense. *See* Ferguson Mun. Code § 29-82 (prohibiting certain conduct that "unreasonably and knowingly disturbs or alarms another person or persons"). Nonetheless, a supervisor approved it. These warrantless arrests violated the Fourth Amendment because they were not based on probable cause. *See Virginia v. Moore*, 553 U.S. 164, 173 (2008).

While the record demonstrates a pattern of stops that are improper from the beginning, it also exposes encounters that start as constitutionally defensible but quickly cross the line. For example, in the summer of 2012, an officer detained a 32-year-old African-American man who was sitting in his car cooling off after playing basketball. The officer arguably had grounds to stop and question the man, since his windows appeared more deeply tinted than permitted under Ferguson's code. Without cause, the officer went on to accuse the man of being a pedophile, prohibit the man from using his cell phone, order the man out of his car for a pat-down despite having no reason to believe he was armed, and ask to search his car. When the man refused, citing his constitutional rights, the officer reportedly pointed a gun at his head, and arrested him. The officer charged the man with eight different counts, including making a false declaration for initially providing the short form of his first name (e.g., "Mike" instead of "Michael") and an address that, although legitimate, differed from the one on his license. The officer also charged the man both with having an

expired operator's license, and with having no operator's license in possession. The man told us he lost his job as a contractor with the federal government as a result of the charges.

b. FPD Officers Routinely Abuse the "Failure to Comply" Charge

One area of FPD activity deserves special attention for its frequency of
Fourth Amendment violations: enforcement of Ferguson's Failure to Comply municipal ordinance.[14] Ferguson Mun. Code § 29-16. Officers rely heavily on this charge to arrest individuals who do not do what they ask, even
when refusal is not a crime. The offense is typically charged under one of
two subsections. One subsection prohibits disobeying a lawful order in a
way that hinders an officer's duties, § 29-16(1); the other requires individuals
to identify themselves, § 29-16(2). FPD engages in a pattern of unconstitutional enforcement with respect to both, resulting in many unlawful arrests.

*i. Improper Enforcement of Code Provision Prohibiting Disobeying a
Lawful Order*

Officers frequently arrest individuals under Section 29-16(1) on facts
that do not meet the provision's elements. Section 29-16(1) makes it unlawful to "[f]ail to comply with the lawful order or request of a police officer
in the discharge of the officer's official duties where such failure interfered
with, obstructed or hindered the officer in the performance of such duties."
Many cases initiated under this provision begin with an officer ordering an
individual to stop despite lacking objective indicia that the individual is engaged in wrongdoing. The order to stop is not a "lawful order" under those
circumstances because the officer lacks reasonable suspicion that criminal
activity is afoot. *See United States v. Brignoni-Ponce*, 422 U.S. 873, 882–83
(1975); *United States v. Jones*, 606 F.3d 964, 967-68 (8th Cir. 2010). Nonetheless, when individuals do not stop in those situations, FPD officers treat
that conduct as a failure to comply with a lawful order, and make arrests.
Such arrests violate the Fourth Amendment because they are not based on
probable cause that the crime of Failure to Comply has been committed.
Dunaway v. New York, 442 U.S. 200, 208 (1979).

FPD officers apply Section 29-16(1) remarkably broadly. In an incident from August 2010, an officer broke up an altercation between two minors and sent them back to their homes. The officer ordered one to stay inside her residence and the other not to return to the first's residence. Later that day, the two minors again engaged in an altercation outside the first minor's residence. The officer arrested both for Failure to Comply with the earlier orders. But Section 29-16(1) does not confer on officers the power to confine people to their homes or keep them away from certain places based solely on their verbal orders. At any rate, the facts of this incident do not satisfy the statute for another reason: there was no evidence that the failure to comply "interfered with, obstructed or hindered the officer in the performance" of official duties. § 29-16(1). The officer's arrest of the two minors for Failure to Comply without probable cause of all elements of the offense violated the Fourth Amendment.

ii. Improper Enforcement of Code Provision Requiring Individuals to Identify Themselves to a Police Officer

FPD's charging under Section 29-16(2) also violates the Constitution. Section 29-16(2) makes it unlawful to "[f]ail to give information requested by a police officer in the discharge of his/her official duties relating to the identity of such person." This provision, a type of "stop-and-identify" law, is likely unconstitutional under the void-for-vagueness doctrine. It is also unconstitutional as typically applied by FPD.

As the Supreme Court has explained, the void-for-vagueness doctrine "requires that a penal statute define the criminal offense with sufficient definiteness that ordinary people can understand what conduct is prohibited and in a manner that does not encourage arbitrary and discriminatory enforcement." *Kolender v. Lawson*, 461 U.S. 352, 357 (1983). In *Kolender*, the Supreme Court invalidated a California stop-and-identify law as unconstitutionally vague because its requirement that detained persons give officers "credible and reliable" identification provided no standard for what a suspect must do to comply with it. Instead, the law "vest[ed] complete discretion in the hands of the police" to determine whether a person had provided sufficient identity information, which created a "potential for arbitrarily suppressing First Amendment liberties" and "the constitutional right to freedom of movement." *Id.* at 358. The Eighth Circuit has applied the doctrine numerous times. In *Fields v. City of Omaha*, 810 F.2d 830 (8th Cir. 1987), the court struck down a city ordinance that required a person to "identify himself" because it did not make definite what would suffice for identification and thereby provided no "standard to guide the police officer's discretionary assessment" or "prevent arbitrary and discriminatory law enforcement." *Id.* at 833–34; *see also Stahl v. City of St. Louis*, 687 F.3d 1038, 1040 (8th Cir. 2012) (holding that an ordinance prohibiting conduct that would impede traffic was unconstitutionally vague under the Due Process Clause because it "may fail to provide the kind of notice that will enable ordinary people to understand what conduct it prohibits") (internal quotation marks omitted).

Under these binding precedents, Ferguson's stop-and-identify law appears to be unconstitutionally vague because the term "information . . . relating to the identity of such person" in Section 29-16(2) is not defined. Neither the ordinance nor any court has narrowed that language. Cf. *Hiibel v. Sixth Judicial Dist. Ct. of Nevada*, 542 U.S. 177, 188–89 (2004) (upholding stop-and-identify law that was construed by the state supreme court to require only that a suspect provide his name). As a consequence, the average person has no understanding of precisely how much identity information, and what kind, he or she must provide when an FPD officer demands it; nor do officers. Indeed, we are aware of several people who were asked to provide their Social Security numbers, including one man who was arrested after refusing to do so. Given that the ordinance appears to lend itself to such arbitrary enforcement, Section 29-16(2) is likely unconstitutional on its face.[15]

Even apart from the facial unconstitutionality of the statute, the evidence is clear that FPD's enforcement of Section 29-16(2) is unconstitutional in its application. Stop-and-identify laws stand in tension with the Supreme Court's admonition that a person approached by a police officer "need not answer any question put to him; indeed, he may decline to listen to the questions at all and may go on his way." *Florida v. Royer*, 460 U.S. 491, 497–98 (1983). For this reason, the Court has held that an officer cannot require a person to identify herself unless the officer first has reasonable suspicion to initiate the stop. *See Brown v. Texas*, 443 U.S. 47, 52–53 (1979) (holding that the application of a Texas statute that criminalized refusal to provide a name and address to a peace officer violated the Fourth Amendment where the officer lacked reasonable suspicion of criminal activity); *see also Hiibel*, 542 U.S. at 184 (deeming the reasonable suspicion requirement a "constitutional limitation[]" on stop-and-identify statutes). FPD officers, however, routinely arrest individuals under Section 29-16(2) for failure to identify themselves despite lacking reasonable suspicion to stop them in the first place.

For example, in an October 2011 incident, an officer arrested two sisters who were backing their car into their driveway. The officer claimed that the car had been idling in the middle of the street, warranting investigation, while the women claim they had pulled up outside their home to drop someone off when the officer arrived. In any case, the officer arrested one sister for failing to provide her identification when requested. He arrested the other sister for getting out of the car after being ordered to stay inside. The two sisters spent the next three hours in jail. In a similar incident from December 2011, police officers approached two people sitting in a car on a public street and asked the driver for identification. When the driver balked, insisting that he was on a public street and should not have to answer questions, the officers ordered him out of the car and ultimately charged him with Failure to Comply.

In another case, from March 2013, officers responded to the police station to take custody of a person wanted on a state warrant. When they arrived, they encountered a different man—not the subject of the warrant—who happened to be leaving the station. Having nothing to connect the man to the warrant subject, other than his presence at the station, the officers nonetheless stopped him and asked that he identify himself. The man asserted his rights, asking the officers "Why do you need to know?" and declining to be frisked. When the man then extended his identification toward the officers, at their request, the officers interpreted his hand motion as an attempted assault and took him to the ground. Without articulating reasonable suspicion or any other justification for the initial detention, the officers arrested the man on two counts of Failure to Comply and two counts of Resisting Arrest.

In our conversations with FPD officers, one officer admitted that when he conducts a traffic stop, he asks for identification from all passengers as a matter of course. If any refuses, he considers that to be "furtive and aggressive" conduct and cites—and typically arrests—the person for Failure to Comply. The officer thus acknowledged that he regularly exceeds his authority under the Fourth Amendment by arresting passengers who refuse, as is their right, to provide identification. *See Hiibel*, 542 U.S. at 188 ("[A]n officer may not arrest a suspect for failure to identify himself if the request for identification is not reasonably related to the circumstances justifying the stop."); *Stufflebeam v. Harris*, 521 F.3d 884, 887–88 (8th Cir. 2008) (holding that the arrest of a passenger for failure to identify himself during a traffic stop violated the Fourth Amendment where the passenger was not suspected of other criminal activity and his identification was not needed for officer safety). Further, the officer told us that he was trained to arrest for this violation.

Good supervision would correct improper arrests by an officer before they became routine. But in Ferguson, the same dynamics that lead officers to make unlawful stops and arrests cause supervisors to conduct only perfunctory review of officers' actions—when they conduct any review at all. FPD supervisors are more concerned with the number of citations and arrests officers produce than whether those citations and arrests are lawful or promote public safety. Internal communications among command staff reveal that FPD for years has failed to ensure even that officers write their reports and first-line supervisors approve them. In 2010, a senior police official complained to supervisors that every week reports go unwritten, and hundreds of reports remain unapproved. "It is time for you to hold your officers accountable," he urged them. In 2014, the official had the same complaint, remarking on 600 reports that had not been approved over a six-month period. Another supervisor remarked that coding errors in the new records management system is set up "to hide, do away with, or just forget reports," creating a heavy administrative burden for supervisors who discover incomplete reports months after they are created. In practice, not all arrests are given incident numbers, meaning supervisors may never know to review them. These systemic deficiencies in oversight are consistent with an approach to law enforcement in which productivity and revenue generation, rather than lawful policing, are the priority. Thus, even as commanders exhort line supervisors to more closely supervise officer activity, they perpetuate the dynamics that discourage meaningful supervision.

c. FPD's Use of a Police-run "Wanted" System Circumvents Judicial Review and Poses the Risk of Abuse

FPD and other law enforcement agencies in St. Louis County use a system of "wanteds" or "stop orders" as a substitute for seeking judicial approval for an arrest warrant. When officers believe a person has committed a crime but are not able to immediately locate that person, they can enter a "wanted" into the statewide law enforcement database, indicating to all other law enforcement agencies that the person should be arrested if located. While wanteds are supposed to be based on probable cause, *see* FPD General Order 424.01, they operate as an end-run around the judicial system. Instead of swearing out a warrant and seeking judicial authorization from a neutral and detached magistrate, officers make the probable cause determination themselves and circumvent the courts. Officers use wanteds for serious state-level crimes and minor code violations alike, including traffic offenses.

FPD command staff express support for the wanted system, extolling the benefits of being able to immediately designate a person for detention. But this expedience carries constitutional risks. If officers enter wanteds into the system on less than probable cause, then the subsequent arrest would violate the Fourth Amendment. Our interviews with command staff and officers indicate that officers do not clearly understand the legal authority necessary to issue a wanted. For example, one veteran officer told us he will put out a wanted "if I do not have enough probable cause to arrest you." He gave the example of investigating a car theft. Upon identifying a suspect, he would put that suspect into the system as wanted "because we do not have probable cause that he stole the vehicle." Reflecting the muddled analysis officers may employ when deciding whether to issue a wanted, this officer concluded, "you have to have reasonable suspicion and some probable cause to put out a wanted."

At times, FPD officers use wanteds not merely in spite of a lack of probable cause, but because they lack probable cause. In December 2014, a Ferguson detective investigating a shooting emailed a county prosecutor to see if a warrant for a suspect could be obtained, since "a lot of state agencies won't act on a wanted." The prosecutor responded stating that although "[c]hances are" the crime was committed by the suspect, "we just don't have enough for a warrant right now." The detective responded that he would enter a wanted.

There is evidence that the use of wanteds has resulted in numerous unconstitutional arrests in Ferguson. Internal communications reveal problems with FPD officers arresting individuals on wanteds without first confirming that the wanteds are still valid. In 2010, for instance, an FPD supervisor wrote that "[a]s of late we have had subjects arrested that were wanted for other agencies brought in without being verified first. You guessed it, come to find out they were no longer wanted by the agencies and had to be released." The same supervisor told us that in 2014 he cleared hundreds of invalid wanteds from the system, some of them over ten years old, suggesting that invalid wanteds have been an ongoing problem.

Wanteds can also be imprecise, leading officers to arrest in violation of the Fourth Amendment. For example, in June 2011, officers arrested a man at gunpoint because the car he was driving had an active wanted "on the vehicle and its occupants" in connection with an alleged theft. In fact, the theft was alleged to have been committed by the man's brother. Nonetheless, according to FPD's files, the man was arrested solely on the basis of the wanted.

This system creates the risk that wanteds could be used improperly to develop evidence necessary for arrest rather than to secure a person against whom probable cause already exists. Several officers described wanteds as an investigatory tool. According to Chief Jackson, "a wanted allows us to get a suspect in for booking and potential interrogation." One purpose, he said, is "to conduct an interview of that person." While it is perfectly legitimate for officers to try to obtain statements from persons lawfully detained, it is unconstitutional for them to jail individuals on less than probable cause for that purpose. *Dunaway*, 442 U.S. at 216. One senior supervisor acknowledged that wanteds could be abused. He agreed that the potential exists, for example, for an officer to pressure a subject into speaking voluntarily to avoid being arrested. These are risks that the judicially-reviewed warrant process is meant to avoid.

Compounding our concern is the minimal training and supervision provided on when to issue a wanted, and the lack of any meaningful oversight to detect and respond to improperly issued wanteds. Some officers told us that they may have heard about wanteds in the training academy. Others said that they received no formal training on wanteds and learned about them from their field training officers. As for supervision, officers are supposed to get authorization from their supervisors before entering a wanted into a law enforcement database. They purportedly do this by providing the factual basis for probable cause to their supervisors, orally or in their written reports. However, several supervisors and officers we spoke with acknowledged that this supervisory review routinely does not happen. Further, the supervisors we interviewed told us that they had never declined to authorize a wanted.

Finally, a Missouri appellate court has highlighted the constitutional risks of relying on a wanted as the basis for an arrest. In *State v. Carroll*, 745 S.W.2d 156 (Mo. Ct. App. 1987), the court held that a robbery suspect was arrested without probable cause when Ferguson and St. Louis police officers picked him up on a wanted for leaving the scene of an accident. *Id.* at 158. The officers then interrogated him three times at two different police stations, and he eventually made incriminating statements. Despite the existence of a wanted, the court deemed the initial arrest unconstitutional because "[t]he record . . . fail[ed] to show any *facts* known to the police at the time of the arrest to support a reasonable belief that defendant had committed a crime." *Id.* *Carroll* highlights the fact that wanteds do not confer an authority equal to a judicial arrest warrant. Rather, the Carroll court's holding suggests that wanteds may be of unknown reliability and thus insufficient to permit custodial detention under the Fourth Amendment. *See also* Steven J. Mulroy, *"Hold" On: The Remarkably Resilient, Constitutionally Dubious 48-Hour Hold,* 63 Case W. Res. L. Rev. 815, 823, 842–45 (2013) (observing that one problem with police "holds" is that, although they require probable cause, "in practice they often lack it").

We received complaints from FPD officers that the County prosecutor's office is too restrictive in granting warrant requests, and that this has necessitated the wanted practice. This investigation did not determine whether the St. Louis County prosecutor is overly restrictive or appropriately cautious in granting warrant requests. What is clear, however, is that current FPD practices have resulted in wanteds being issued and executed without legal basis.

2. FPD ENGAGES IN A PATTERN OF FIRST AMENDMENT VIOLATIONS

FPD's approach to enforcement results in violations of individuals' First Amendment rights. FPD arrests people for a variety of protected conduct: people are punished for talking back to officers, recording public police activities, and lawfully protesting perceived injustices.

Under the Constitution, what a person says generally should not determine whether he or she is jailed. Police officers cannot constitutionally make arrest decisions based on individuals' verbal expressions of disrespect for law enforcement, including use of foul language. *Buffkins v. City of Omaha,* 922 F.2d 465, 472 (8th Cir. 1990) (holding that officers violated the Constitution when they arrested a woman for disorderly conduct after she called one an "asshole," especially since "police officers are expected to exercise greater restraint in their response than the average citizen"); *Copeland v. Locke,* 613 F.3d 875, 880 (8th Cir. 2010) (holding that the First Amendment prohibited a police chief from arresting an individual who pointed at him and told him "move the f*****g car," even if the comment momentarily distracted the chief from a routine traffic stop); *Gorra v. Hanson*, 880 F.2d 95, 100 (8th Cir. 1989) (holding that arresting a person in retaliation for making a statement "constitutes obvious infringement" of the First Amendment). As the Supreme Court has held, "the First Amendment protects a significant amount of verbal criticism and challenge directed at police officers." *City of Houston, Tex. v. Hill*, 482 U.S. 451, 461 (1987) (striking down as unconstitutionally overbroad a local ordinance that criminalized interference with police by speech).

In Ferguson, however, officers frequently make enforcement decisions based on what subjects say, or how they say it. Just as officers reflexively resort to arrest immediately upon noncompliance with their orders, whether lawful or not, they are quick to overreact to challenges and verbal slights. These incidents—sometimes called "contempt of cop" cases—are propelled by officers' belief that arrest is an appropriate response to disrespect. These arrests are typically charged as a Failure to Comply, Disorderly Conduct, Interference with Officer, or Resisting Arrest.

For example, in July 2012, a police officer arrested a business owner on charges of Interfering in Police Business and Misuse of 911 because she objected to the officer's detention of her employee. The officer had stopped the employee for "walking unsafely in the street" as he returned to work from the bank. According to FPD records, the owner "became verbally involved," came out of her shop three times after being asked to stay inside, and called 911 to complain to the Police Chief. The officer characterized her protestations as interference and arrested her inside her shop.[16] The arrest violated the First Amendment, which "does not allow such speech to be made a crime." *Hill*, 482 U.S. at 462. Indeed, the officer's decision to arrest the woman after she tried to contact the Police Chief suggests that he may have been retaliating against her for reporting his conduct.

Officers in Ferguson also use their arrest power to retaliate against individuals for using language that, while disrespectful, is protected by the Constitution. For example, one afternoon in September 2012, an officer stopped a 20-year-old African-American man for dancing in the middle of a residential street. The officer obtained the man's identification and ran his name for warrants. Finding none, he told the man he was free to go. The man responded with profanities. When the officer told him to watch his language and reminded him that he was not being arrested, the man continued using profanity and was arrested for Manner of Walking in Roadway.

In February 2014, officers responded to a group of African-American teenage girls "play fighting" (in the words of the officer) in an intersection after school. When one of the schoolgirls gave the middle finger to a white witness who had called the police, an officer ordered her over to him. One of the girl's friends accompanied her. Though the friend had the right to be present and observe the situation—indeed, the offense reports include no facts suggesting a safety concern posed by her presence—the officers ordered her to leave and then attempted to arrest her when she refused. Officers used force to arrest the friend as she pulled away. When the first girl grabbed an officer's shoulder, they used force to arrest her, as well. Officers charged the two teenagers with a variety of offenses, including: Disorderly Conduct for giving the middle finger and using obscenities; Manner of Walking for being in the street; Failure to Comply for staying to observe; Interference with Officer; Assault on a Law Enforcement Officer; and Endangering the Welfare of a Child (themselves and their schoolmates) by resisting arrest and being involved in disorderly conduct. This incident underscores how officers' unlawful response to activity protected by the First Amendment can quickly escalate to physical resistance, resulting in additional force, additional charges, and increasing the risk of injury to officers and members of the public alike.

These accounts are drawn entirely from officers' own descriptions, recorded in offense reports. That FPD officers believe criticism and insolence are grounds for arrest, and that supervisors have condoned such unconstitutional policing, reflects intolerance for even lawful opposition to the exercise of police authority. These arrests also reflect that, in FPD, many officers have no tools for de-escalating emotionally charged scenes, even though the ability of a police officer to bring calm to a situation is a core policing skill.

FPD officers also routinely infringe on the public's First Amendment rights by preventing people from recording their activities. The First Amendment "prohibit[s] the government from limiting the stock of information from which members of the public may draw." *First Nat'l Bank v. Belloti*, 435 U.S. 765, 783 (1978). Applying this principle, the federal courts of appeal have held that the First Amendment "unambiguously" establishes a constitutional right to videotape police activities. *Glik v. Cunniffe*, 655 F.3d 78, 82 (1st Cir. 2011); *see also ACLU v. Alvarez*, 679 F.3d 583, 600 (7th Cir. 2012) (issuing a preliminary injunction against the use of a state eavesdropping statute to prevent the recording of public police activities); *Fordyce v. City of Seattle*, 55 F.3d 436, 439 (9th Cir. 1995) (recognizing a First Amendment right to film police carrying out their public duties); *Smith v. City of Cumming*, 212 F.3d 1332, 1333 (11th Cir. 2000) (recognizing a First Amendment right "to photograph or videotape police conduct"). Indeed, as the ability to record police activity has become more widespread, the role it can play in capturing questionable police activity, and ensuring that the activity is investigated and subject to broad public debate, has become clear. Protecting civilian recording of police activity is thus at the core of speech the First Amendment is intended to protect. *Cf. Branzburg v. Hayes*, 408 U.S. 665, 681 (1972) (First Amendment protects "news gathering"); *Mills v. Alabama*, 384 U.S. 214, 218 (1966) (news gathering enhances "free discussion of governmental affairs"). "In a democracy, public officials have no general privilege to avoid publicity and embarrassment by preventing public scrutiny of their actions." *Walker v. City of Pine Bluff*, 414 F.3d 989, 992 (8th Cir. 2005).

In Ferguson, however, officers claim without any factual support that the use of camera phones endangers officer safety. Sometimes, officers offer no rationale at all. Our conversations with community members and review of FPD records found numerous violations of the right to record police activity. In May 2014, an officer pulled over an African-American woman who was driving with her two sons. During the traffic stop, the woman's 16-year-old son began recording with his cell phone. The officer ordered him to put down the phone and refrain from using it for the remainder of the stop. The officer claimed this was "for safety reasons." The situation escalated, apparently due to the officer's rudeness and the woman's response. According to the 16 year old, he began recording again, leading the officer to wrestle the phone from him. Additional officers arrived and used force to arrest all three civilians under disputed circumstances that could have been clarified by a video recording.

In June 2014, an African-American couple who had taken their children to play at the park allowed their small children to urinate in the bushes next to their parked car. An officer stopped them, threatened to cite them for allowing the children to "expose themselves," and checked the father for warrants. When the mother asked if the officer had to detain the father in front of the children, the officer turned to the father and said, "you're going to jail because your wife keeps running her mouth." The mother then began recording the officer on her cell phone. The officer became irate, declaring, "you don't videotape me!" As the officer drove away with the father in custody for "parental neglect," the mother drove after them, continuing to record. The officer then pulled over and arrested her for traffic violations. When the father asked the officer to show mercy, he responded, "no more mercy, since she wanted to videotape," and declared "nobody videotapes me." The officer then took the phone, which the couple's daughter was holding. After posting bond, the couple found that the video had been deleted.

A month later, the same officer pulled over a truck hauling a trailer that did not have operating tail lights. The officer asked for identification from all three people inside, including a 54-year-old white man in the passenger seat who asked why. "You have to have a reason. This is a violation of my Fourth Amendment rights," he asserted. The officer, who characterized the man's reaction as "suspicious," responded, "the reason is, if you don't hand it to me, I'll arrest you." The man provided his identification. The officer then asked the man to move his cell phone from his lap to the dashboard, "for my safety." The man said, "okay, but I'm going to record this." Due to nervousness, he could not open the recording application and quickly placed the phone on the dash. The officer then announced that the man was under arrest for Failure to Comply. At the end of the traffic stop, the officer gave the driver a traffic citation, indicated at the other man, and said, "you're getting this ticket because of him." Upon bringing that man to the jail, someone asked the officer what offense the man had committed. The officer responded, "he's one of those guys who watches CNBC too much about his rights." The man did not say anything else, fearing what else the officer might be capable of doing. He later told us, "I never dreamed I could end up in jail for this. I'm scared of driving through Ferguson now."

The Ferguson Police Department's infringement of individuals' freedom of speech and right to record has been highlighted in recent months in the context of large-scale public protest. In November 2014, a federal judge entered a consent order prohibiting Ferguson officers from interfering with individuals' rights to lawfully and peacefully record public police activities. That same month, the City settled another suit alleging that it had abused its loitering ordinance, Mun. Code § 29-89, to arrest people who were protesting peacefully on public sidewalks.

Despite these lawsuits, it appears that FPD continues to interfere with individuals' rights to protest and record police activities. On February 9, 2015, several individuals were protesting outside the Ferguson police station on the six-month anniversary of Michael Brown's death. According to protesters, and consistent with several video recordings from that evening, the protesters stood peacefully in the police department's parking lot, on the sidewalks in front of it, and across the street. Video footage shows that two FPD vehicles abruptly accelerated from the police parking lot into the street. An officer announced, "everybody here's going to jail," causing the protesters to run. Video shows that as one man recorded the police arresting others, he was arrested for interfering with police action. Officers pushed him to the ground, began handcuffing him, and announced, "stop resisting or you're going to get tased." It appears from the video, however, that the man was neither interfering nor resisting. A protester in a wheelchair who was live streaming the protest was also arrested. Another officer moved several people with cameras away from the scene of the arrests, warning them against interfering and urging them to back up or else be arrested for

Failure to Obey. The sergeant shouted at those filming that they would be arrested for Manner of Walking if they did not back away out of the street, even though it appears from the video recordings that the protesters and those recording were on the sidewalk at most, if not all, times. Six people were arrested during this incident. It appears that officers' escalation of this incident was unnecessary and in response to derogatory comments written in chalk on the FPD parking lot asphalt and on a police vehicle.

FPD's suppression of speech reflects a police culture that relies on the exercise of police power—however unlawful—to stifle unwelcome criticism. Recording police activity and engaging in public protest are fundamentally democratic enterprises because they provide a check on those "who are granted substantial discretion that may be misused to deprive individuals of their liberties." *Glik*, 655 F.3d at 82. Even profane backtalk can be a form of dissent against perceived misconduct. In the words of the Supreme Court, "[t]he freedom of individuals verbally to oppose or challenge police action without thereby risking arrest is one of the principal characteristics by which we distinguish a free nation from a police state." *Hill*, 482 U.S. at 463. Ideally, officers would not encounter verbal abuse. Communities would encourage mutual respect, and the police would likewise exhibit respect by treating people with dignity. But, particularly where officers engage in unconstitutional policing, they only exacerbate community opposition by quelling speech.

3. FPD ENGAGES IN A PATTERN OF EXCESSIVE FORCE IN VIOLATION OF THE FOURTH AMENDMENT

FPD engages in a pattern of excessive force in violation of the Fourth Amendment. Many officers are quick to escalate encounters with subjects they perceive to be disobeying their orders or resisting arrest. They have come to rely on ECWs, specifically Tasers®, where less force—or no force at all—would do. They also release canines on unarmed subjects unreasonably and before attempting to use force less likely to cause injury. Some incidents of excessive force result from stops or arrests that have no basis in law. Others are punitive and retaliatory. In addition, FPD records suggest a tendency to use unnecessary force against vulnerable groups such as people with mental health conditions or cognitive disabilities, and juvenile students. Furthermore, as discussed in greater detail in Part III.C. of this report, Ferguson's pattern of using excessive force disproportionately harms African-American members of the community. The overwhelming majority of force—almost 90%—is used against African Americans.

The use of excessive force by a law enforcement officer violates the Fourth Amendment. *Graham v. Conner*, 490 U.S. 386, 394 (1989); *Atkinson v. City of Mountain View, Mo.*, 709 F.3d 1201, 1207–09 (8th Cir. 2013). The constitutionality of an officer's use of force depends on whether the officer's conduct was "'objectively reasonable' in light of the facts and circumstances," which must be assessed "from the perspective of a reasonable officer on the scene, rather than with the 20/20 vision of hindsight." *Graham*, 490 U.S. at 396. Relevant considerations include "the severity of the crime at issue, whether the suspect poses an immediate threat to the safety of the officers or others, and whether he is actively resisting arrest or attempting to evade arrest by flight." *Id.*; *Johnson v. Caroll*, 658 F.3d 819, 826 (8th Cir. 2011).

FPD also imposes limits on officers' use of force through department policies. The use-of-force policy instituted by Chief Jackson in 2010 states that "force may not be resorted to unless other reasonable alternatives have been exhausted or would clearly be ineffective under a particular set of circumstances." FPD General Order 410.01. The policy also sets out a use-of-force continuum, indicating the force options permitted in different circumstances, depending on the level of resistance provided by a suspect. FPD General Order 410.08.

FPD's stated practice is to maintain use-of-force investigation files for all situations in which officers use force. We reviewed the entire set of force files provided by the department for the period of January 1, 2010 to September 8, 2014.[17] Setting aside the killing of animals (e.g., dogs, injured deer) and three instances in which the subject of the use of force was not identified, FPD provided 151 files. We also reviewed related documentation regarding canine deployments. Our finding that FPD force is routinely unreasonable and sometimes clearly punitive is drawn largely from FPD's documentation; that is, from officers' own words.

a. FPD's Use of Electronic Control Weapons Is Unreasonable

FPD's pattern of excessive force includes using ECWs in a manner that is unconstitutional, abusive, and unsafe. For example, in August 2010, a lieutenant used an ECW in drive-stun mode against an African-American woman in the Ferguson City Jail because she had refused to remove her bracelets.[18] The lieutenant resorted to his ECW even though there were five officers present and the woman posed no physical threat.

Similarly, in November 2013, a correctional officer fired an ECW at an African-American woman's chest because she would not follow his verbal commands to walk toward a cell. The woman, who had been arrested for driving while intoxicated, had yelled an insulting remark at the officer, but her conduct amounted to verbal noncompliance or passive resistance at most. Instead of attempting hand controls or seeking assistance from a state trooper who was also present, the correctional officer deployed the ECW because the woman was "not doing as she was told." When another FPD officer wrote up the formal incident report, the reporting officer wrote that the woman "approached [the correctional officer] in a threatening manner." This "threatening manner" allegation appears nowhere in the statements of the correctional officer or witness trooper. The woman was charged with Disorderly Conduct, and the correctional officer soon went on to become an officer with another law enforcement agency.

These are not isolated incidents. In September 2012, an officer drive-stunned an African-American woman who he had placed in the back of his patrol car but who had stretched out her leg to block him from closing the door. The woman was in handcuffs. In May 2013, officers drive-stunned a handcuffed African-American man who verbally refused to get out of the back seat of a police car once it had arrived at the jail. The man did not physically resist arrest or attempt to assault the officers. According to the man, he was also punched in the face and head. That allegation was neither reported by the involved officers nor investigated by their supervisor, who dismissed it.

FPD officers seem to regard ECWs as an all-purpose tool bearing no risk. But an ECW—an electroshock weapon that disrupts a person's muscle control, causing involuntary contractions—can indeed be harmful. The Eighth Circuit Court of Appeals has observed that ECW-inflicted injuries are "sometimes severe and unexpected." *LaCross v. City of Duluth*, 713 F.3d 1155, 1158 (8th Cir. 2013). Electroshock "inflicts a painful and frightening blow, which temporarily paralyzes the large muscles of the body, rendering the victim helpless." *Hickey v. Reeder*, 12 F.3d 754, 757 (8th Cir. 1993). Guidance produced by the United States Department of Justice, Office of Community Oriented Policing Services, and the Police Executive Research Forum in 2011 warns that ECWs are "'less-lethal' and not 'non-lethal weapons'" and "have the potential to result in a fatal outcome." *2011 Electronic Control Weapon Guidelines*, 12 (Police Executive Research Forum & U.S. Dep't of Justice Office of Community Oriented Policing Services, Mar. 2011) (*"2011 ECW Guidelines"*).

FPD officers' swift, at times automatic, resort to using ECWs against individuals who typically have committed low-level crimes and who pose no immediate threat violates the Constitution. As the Eighth Circuit held in 2011, an officer uses excessive force and violates clearly established Fourth Amendment law when he deploys an ECW against an individual whose crime was minor and who is not actively resisting, attempting to flee, or posing any imminent danger to others. *Brown v. City of Golden Valley*, 574 F.3d 491, 497–99 (8th Cir. 2011) (upholding the denial of a qualified immunity claim made by an officer who drive-stunned a woman on her arm for two or three seconds when she refused to hang up her phone despite being ordered to do so twice); *cf. Hickey*, 12 F.3d at 759 (finding that the use of a stun gun against a prisoner for refusing to sweep his cell violated the more deferential Eighth Amendment prohibition against cruel and unusual punishment). Courts have found that even when a suspect resists but does so only minimally, the surrounding factors may render the use of an ECW objectively unreasonable. *See Mattos v. Agarano*, 661 F.3d 433, 444–

46, 448–51 (9th Cir. 2011) (en banc) (holding in two consolidated cases that minimal defensive resistance—including stiffening the body to inhibit being pulled from a car, and raising an arm in defense—does not render using an ECW reasonable where the offense was minor, the subject did not attempt to flee, and the subject posed no immediate threat to officers); *Parker v. Gerrish*, 547 F.3d 1, 9–11 (1st Cir. 2008) (upholding a jury verdict of excessive use of force for an ECW use because the evidence supported a finding that the subject who had held his hands together was not actively resisting or posing an immediate threat); *Casey v. City of Fed. Heights*, 509 F.3d 1278, 1282–83 (10th Cir. 2007) (holding that the use of an ECW was not objectively reasonable when the subject pulled away from the officer but did not otherwise actively resist arrest, attempt to flee, or pose an immediate threat).

Indeed, officers' unreasonable ECW use violates FPD's own policies. The department prohibits the use of force unless reasonable alternatives have been exhausted or would clearly be ineffective. FPD General Order 410.01. A separate ECW policy describes the weapon as "designed to overcome active aggression or overt actions of assault." FPD General Order 499.00. The policy states that an ECW "will never be deployed punitively or for purposes of coercion. It is to be used as a way of averting a potentially injurious or dangerous situation." FPD General Order 499.04. Despite the existence of clearly established Fourth Amendment case law and explicit departmental policies in this area, FPD officers routinely engage in the unreasonable use of ECWs, and supervisors routinely approve their conduct.

It is in part FPD officers' approach to policing that leads them to violate the Constitution and FPD's own policies. Officers across the country encounter drunkenness, passive defiance, and verbal challenges. But in Ferguson, officers have not been trained or incentivized to use de-escalation techniques to avoid or minimize force in these situations. Instead, they respond with impatience, frustration, and disproportionate force. FPD's weak oversight of officer use of force, described in greater detail below, facilitates this abuse. Officers should be required to view the ECW as one tool among many, and "a weapon of need, not a tool of convenience." *2011*

ECW Guidelines at 11. Effective policing requires that officers not depend on ECWs, or any type of force, "at the expense of diminishing the fundamental skills of communicating with subjects and de-escalating tense encounters." *Id.* at 12.

b. FPD's Use of Canines on Low-level, Unarmed Offenders Is Unreasonable

FPD engages in a pattern of deploying canines to bite individuals when the articulated facts do not justify this significant use of force. The department's own records demonstrate that, as with other types of force, canine officers use dogs out of proportion to the threat posed by the people they encounter, leaving serious puncture wounds to nonviolent offenders, some of them children. Furthermore, in every canine bite incident for which racial information is available, the subject was African American. This disparity, in combination with the decision to deploy canines in circumstances with a seemingly low objective threat, suggests that race may play an impermissible role in officers' decisions to deploy canines.

FPD currently has four canines, each assigned to a particular canine officer. Under FPD policy, canines are to be used to locate and apprehend "dangerous offenders." FPD General Order 498.00. When offenders are hiding, the policy states, "handlers will not allow their K-9 to engage a suspect by biting if a lower level of force could reasonably be expected to control the suspect or allow for the apprehension." *Id.* at 498.06. The policy also permits the use of a canine, however, when any crime—not just a felony or violent crime—has been committed. *Id.* at 498.05. This permissiveness, combined with the absence of meaningful supervisory review and an apparent tendency to overstate the threat based on race, has resulted in avoidable dog bites to low-level offenders when other means of control were available.

In December 2011, officers deployed a canine to bite an unarmed 14-year-old African-American boy who was waiting in an abandoned house for his friends. Four officers, including a canine officer, responded to the house mid-morning after a caller reported that people had gone inside. Officers arrested one boy on the ground level. Describing the offense as a burglary in progress even though the facts showed that the only plausible offense was trespassing, the canine officer's report stated that the dog located a second boy hiding in a storage closet under the stairs in the basement. The officer peeked into the space and saw the boy, who was 5'5" and 140 pounds, curled up in a ball, hiding. According to the officer, the boy would not show his hands despite being warned that the officer would use the dog. The officer then deployed the dog, which bit the boy's arm, causing puncture wounds.

According to the boy, with whom we spoke, he never hid in a storage space and he never heard any police warnings. He told us that he was waiting for his friends in the basement of the house, a vacant building where they would go when they skipped school. The boy approached the stairs when he heard footsteps on the upper level, thinking his friends had arrived. When he saw the dog at the top of the steps, he turned to run, but the dog quickly bit him on the ankle and then the thigh, causing him to fall to the floor. The dog was about to bite his face or neck but instead got his left arm, which the boy had raised to protect himself. FPD officers struck him while he was on the ground, one of them putting a boot on the side of his head. He recalled the officers laughing about the incident afterward.

The lack of sufficient documentation or a supervisory force investigation prevents us from resolving which version of events is more accurate. However, even if the officer's version of the force used were accurate, the use of the dog to bite the boy was unreasonable. Though described as a felony, the facts as described by the officer, and the boy, indicate that this was a trespass—kids hanging out in a vacant building. The officers had no factual predicate to believe the boy was armed. The offense reports document no attempt to glean useful information about the second boy from the first, who was quickly arrested. By the canine officer's own account, he saw the boy in the closet and thus had the opportunity to assess the threat posed by this 5'5" 14 year old. Moreover, there were no exigent circumstances requiring apprehension by dog bite. Four officers were present and had control of the scene.

There is a recurring pattern of officers claiming they had to use a canine to extract a suspect hiding in a closed space. The frequency with which this particular rationale is used to justify dog bites, alongside the conclusory language in the reports, provides cause for concern. In December 2012, a 16-year-old African-American boy suspected of stealing a car fled from an officer, jumped several fences, and ran into a vacant house. A second officer arrived with a canine, which reportedly located the suspect hiding in a closet. Without providing a warning outside the closet, the officer opened the door and sent in the dog, which bit the suspect and dragged him out by the legs. This force appears objectively unreasonable. *See Kuha v. City of Minnetonka*, 365 F.3d 590, 598 (8th Cir. 2004), abrogated on other grounds by *Szabla v. City of Brooklyn Park, Minn.*, 486 F.3d 385, 396 (8th Cir. 2007) (en banc) (holding that "a jury could find it objectively unreasonable to use a police dog trained in the bite and hold method without first giving the suspect a warning and opportunity for peaceful surrender"). The first officer, who was also on the scene by this point, deployed his ECW against the suspect three times as the suspect struggled with the dog, which was still biting him. The offense reports provide only minimal explanation for why apprehension by dog bite was necessary. The pursuing officer claimed the suspect had "reached into the front section of his waist area," but the report does not say that he relayed this information to the canine officer, and no weapon was found. Moreover, given the lack of a warning at the closet, the use of the dog and ECW at the same time, and the application of three ECW stuns in quick succession, the officers' conduct raises the possibility that the force was applied in retaliation for leading officers on a chase.

In November 2013, an officer deployed a canine to bite and detain a fleeing subject even though the officer knew the suspect was unarmed. The officer deemed the subject, an African-American male who was walking down the street, suspicious because he appeared to walk away when he saw the officer. The officer stopped him and frisked him, finding no weapons. The officer then ran his name for warrants. When the man heard the dispatcher say over the police radio that he had outstanding warrants—the report does not specify whether the warrants were for failing to appear in municipal court or to pay owed fines, or something more serious—he ran.

The sergeant detained the man, although he did not articulate any reasonable suspicion that criminal activity was afoot. When the man declined to answer questions or submit to a frisk—which the sergeant sought to execute despite articulating no reason to believe the man was armed—the sergeant grabbed the man by the belt, drew his ECW, and ordered the man to comply. The man crossed his arms and objected that he had not done anything wrong. Video captured by the ECW's built-in camera shows that the man made no aggressive movement toward the officer. The sergeant fired the ECW, applying a five-second cycle of electricity and causing the man to fall to the ground. The sergeant almost immediately applied the ECW again, which he later justified in his report by claiming that the man tried to stand up. The video makes clear, however, that the man never tried to stand—he only writhed in pain on the ground. The video also shows that the sergeant applied the ECW nearly continuously for 20 seconds, longer than represented in his report. The man was charged with Failure to Comply and Resisting Arrest, but no independent criminal violation.

In a January 2014 incident, officers attempted to arrest a young African-American man for trespassing on his girlfriend's grandparents' property, even though the man had been invited into the home by the girlfriend. According to officers, he resisted arrest, requiring several officers to subdue him. Seven officers repeatedly struck and used their ECWs against the subject, who was 5'8" and 170 pounds. The young man suffered head lacerations with significant bleeding.

In the above examples, force resulted from temporary detentions or attempted arrests for which officers lacked legal authority. Force at times appeared to be used as punishment for non-compliance with an order that lacked legal authority. Even where FPD officers have legal grounds to stop or arrest, however, they frequently take actions that ratchet up tensions and needlessly escalate the situation to the point that they feel force is necessary. One illustrative instance from October 2012 began as a purported check on a pedestrian's well-being and ended with the man being taken to the ground, drive-stunned twice, and arrested for Manner of Walking in

Roadway and Failure to Comply. In that case, an African-American man was walking after midnight in the outer lane of West Florissant Avenue when an officer asked him to stop. The officer reported that he believed the man might be under the influence of an "impairing substance." When the man, who was 5'5" and 135 pounds, kept walking, the officer grabbed his arm; when the man pulled away, the officer forced him to the ground. Then, for reasons not articulated in the officer's report, the officer decided to handcuff the man, applying his ECW in drive-stun mode twice, reportedly because the man would not provide his hand for cuffing. The man was arrested but there is no indication in the report that he was in fact impaired or indeed doing anything other than walking down the street when approached by the officer.

In November 2011, officers stopped a car for speeding. The two African-American women inside exited the car and vocally objected to the stop. They were told to get back in the car. When the woman in the passenger seat got out a second time, an officer announced she was under arrest for Failure to Comply. This decision escalated into a use of force. According to the officers, the woman swung her arms and legs, although apparently not at anyone, and then stiffened her body. An officer responded by drive-stunning her in the leg. The woman was charged with Failure to Comply and Resisting Arrest.

As these examples demonstrate, a significant number of the documented use-of-force incidents involve charges of Failure to Comply and Resisting Arrest only. This means that officers who claim to act based on reasonable suspicion or probable cause of a crime either are wrong much of the time or do not have an adequate legal basis for many stops and arrests in the first place. *Cf. Lewis v. City of New Orleans*, 415 U.S. 130, 136 (1974) (Powell, J., concurring) (cautioning that an overbroad code ordinance "tends to be invoked only where there is no other valid basis for arresting an objectionable or suspicious person" and that the "opportunity for abuse . . . is self-evident"). This pattern is a telltale sign of officer escalation and a strong indicator that the use of force was avoidable.

e. FPD Officers Have a Pattern of Resorting to Force Too Quickly When Interacting with Vulnerable Populations

Another dimension of FPD's pattern of unreasonable force is FPD's overreliance on force when interacting with more vulnerable populations, such as people with mental health conditions or intellectual disabilities and juvenile students.

i. Force Used Against People with Mental Health Conditions or Intellectual Disabilities

The Fourth Amendment requires that an individual's mental health condition or intellectual disability be considered when determining the reasonableness of an officer's use of force. *See Champion v. Outlook Nashville, Inc.*, 380 F.3d 893, 904 (6th Cir. 2004) (explaining in case concerning use of force against a detainee with autism that "[t]he diminished capacity of an unarmed detainee must be taken into account when assessing the amount of force exerted"); *see also Phillips v. Community Ins. Corp.*, 678 F.3d 513, 526 (7th Cir. 2012); Deorle v. Rutherford, 272 F.3d 1272, 1283 (9th Cir. 2001); *Giannetti v. City of Stillwater*, 216 F. App'x 756, 764 (10th Cir. 2007). This is because people with such disabilities "may be physically unable to comply with police commands." *Phillips*, 678 F.3d at 526. Our review indicates that FPD officers do not adequately consider the mental health or cognitive disability of those they suspect of wrongdoing when deciding whether to use force.

Ferguson is currently in litigation against the estate of a man with mental illness who died in September 2011 after he had an ECW deployed against him three times for allegedly running toward an officer while swinging his fist. *See Estate of Moore v. Ferguson Police Dep't*, No. 4:14-cv-01443 (E.D. Mo. filed Aug. 19, 2014). The man had been running naked through the streets and pounding on cars that morning while yelling "I am Jesus." The Eighth Circuit recently considered a similar set of allegations in *De Boise v. Taser Intern., Inc.*, 760 F.3d 892 (8th Cir. 2014). There, a man suffering from schizophrenia, who had run naked in and out of his house and claimed to be a god, died after officers used their ECWs against him multiple times because he would not stay on the ground. *Id.* at 897-98. Although the court resolved the case on qualified immunity grounds without deciding the excessive-force issue, the one judge who reached that issue opined that the allegations could be sufficient to establish a Fourth Amendment violation. *Id.* at 899–900 (Bye, J., dissenting).

In 2013, FPD stopped a man running with a shopping cart because he seemed "suspicious." According to the file, the man was "obviously mentally handicapped." Officers took the man to the ground and attempted to arrest him for Failure to Comply after he refused to submit to a pat-down. In the officers' view, the man resisted arrest by pulling his arms away. The officers drive-stunned him in the side of the neck. They charged him only with Failure to Comply and Resisting Arrest. In August 2011, officers used an ECW device against a man with diabetes who bit an EMT's hand without breaking the skin. The man had been having seizures when he did not comply with officer commands.

In August 2010, an officer responded to a call about an African-American man walking onto the highway and lying down on the pavement. Seeing that the man was sweating, acting jittery, and had dilated pupils, the officer believed he was on drugs. The man was cooperative at first but balked, pushing the officer back when the officer tried to handcuff him for safety reasons. The officer struck the man several times with his Asp® baton—including once in the head, a form of deadly force—causing significant bleeding. Two other officers then deployed their ECWs against the man a total of five times.

Jail staff have also reacted to people with mental health conditions by resorting to greater force than necessary. For example, in July 2011, a correctional officer used an ECW to drive-stun an African-American male inmate three times after he tried to hang himself with material torn from a medical dressing and banged his head on the cell wall. That same month, a correctional officer used an ECW against an African-American inmate with bipolar disorder who broke the overhead glass light fixture and tried to use it to cut his wrists. According to the correctional officer, the glass was "safety glass" and could not be used to cut the skin.

These incidents indicate a pattern of insufficient sensitivity to, and training about, the limitations of those with mental health conditions or intellectual disabilities. Officers view mental illness as narcotic intoxication, or worse, willful defiance. They apply excessive force to such subjects, not accounting for the possibility that the subjects may not understand their commands or be able to comply with them. And they have been insufficiently trained on tactics that would minimize force when dealing with individuals who are in mental health crisis or who have intellectual disabilities.

ii. Force Used Against Students

FPD's approach to policing impacts how its officers interact with students, as well, leading them to treat routine discipline issues as criminal matters and to use force when communication and de-escalation techniques would likely resolve the conflict.

FPD stations two School Resource Officers in the Ferguson-Florissant School District,[19] one at Ferguson Middle School and one at McCluer South-Berkeley High School. The stated mission of the SRO program, according to the memorandum of understanding between FPD and the school district, is to provide a safe and secure learning environment for students. But that agreement does not clearly define the SROs' role or limit SRO involvement in cases of routine discipline or classroom management. Nor has FPD established such guidance for its SROs or provided officers with adequate training on engaging with youth in an educational setting. The result of these failures, combined with FPD's culture of unreasonable enforcement actions more generally, is police action that is unreasonable for a school environment.

For example, in November 2013, an SRO charged a ninth grade girl with several violations after she refused to follow his orders to walk to the principal's office. The student and a classmate, both 15-year-old African-American girls, had gotten into a fight during class. When the officer responded, school staff had the two girls separated in a hallway. One refused the officer's order to walk to the principal's office, instead trying to push past staff toward the other girl. The officer pushed her backward toward a row of lockers and then announced that she was under arrest for Failure to Comply. Although the officer agreed not to handcuff her when she agreed to walk to the principals' office, he forwarded charges of Failure to Comply, Resisting Arrest, and Peace Disturbance to the county family court. The other student was charged with Peace Disturbance.

FPD officers respond to misbehavior common among students with arrest and force, rather than reserving arrest for cases involving safety threats. As one SRO told us, the arrests he made during the 2013–14 school year overwhelmingly involved minor offenses—Disorderly Conduct, Peace Disturbance, and Failure to Comply with instructions. In one case, an SRO decided to arrest a 14-year-old African-American student at the Ferguson Middle School for Failure to Comply when the student refused to leave the classroom after getting into a trivial argument with another student. The situation escalated, resulting in the student being drive-stunned with an ECW in the classroom and the school seeking a 180-day suspension for the student. SROs' propensity for arresting students demonstrates a lack of understanding of the negative consequences associated with such arrests. In fact, SROs told us that they viewed increased arrests in the schools as a positive result of their work. This perspective suggests a failure of training (including training in mental health, counseling, and the development of the teenage brain); a lack of priority given to de-escalation and conflict resolution; and insufficient appreciation for the negative educational and long-term outcomes that can result from treating disciplinary concerns as crimes and using force on students. *See* Dear Colleague Letter on the Nondiscriminatory Administration of School Discipline, U.S. Dep't of Justice & U.S. Dep't of Education, http://www.justice.gov/crt/about/edu/documents/dcl.pdf (2014) (citing research and providing guidance to public schools on how to comply with federal nondiscrimination law).

f. FPD's Weak Oversight of Use of Force Reflects its Lack of Concern for Whether Officer Conduct Is Consistent with the Law or Promotes Police Legitimacy

FPD's use-of-force review system is particularly ineffectual. Force frequently is not reported. When it is, there is rarely any meaningful review. Supervisors do little to no investigation; either do not understand or choose not to follow FPD's use-of-force policy in analyzing officer conduct; rarely correct officer misconduct when they find it; and do not see the patterns of abuse that are evident when viewing these incidents in the aggregate.

While Chief Jackson implemented new department policies when he joined FPD in 2010, including on use-of-force reporting and review, these policies are routinely ignored. Under FPD General Order 410.00, when an officer uses or attempts to use any force, a supervisor must respond to the scene to investigate. The supervisor must complete a two-page use-of-force report assessing whether the use of force complied with FPD's force policy. Additional forms are required for ECW uses and vehicle pursuits. According to policy and our interviews with Chief Jackson, a use-of-force packet is assembled—which should include the use-of-force report and supplemental forms, all police reports, any photographs, and any other supporting materials—and forwarded up the chain of command to the Chief. The force reporting and review system is intended to "help identify trends, improve training and officer safety, and provide timely information for the department addressing use-of-force issues with the public." FPD General Order 410.07. The policy even requires that a professional standards officer conduct an annual review of all force incidents. *Id.* These requirements are not adhered to in practice.

Perhaps the greatest deviation from FPD's use-of-force policies is that officers frequently do not report the force they use at all. There are many indications that this underreporting is widespread. First, we located information in FPD's internal affairs files indicating instances of force that were not included in the force files provided by FPD. Second, in reviewing randomly selected reports from FPD's records management system, we found several offense reports that described officers using force with no corresponding use-of-force report. Third, we found evidence that force had been used but not documented in officers' workers compensation claims. Of the nine cases between 2010 and 2014 in which officers claimed injury sustained from using force on the job, three had no corresponding use-of-force paperwork. Fourth, the set of force investigations provided by FPD contains lengthy gaps, including six stretches of time ranging from two to four months in which no incidents of force are reported. Otherwise, the files typically reflect between two and six force incidents per month. Fifth, we heard from community members about uses of force that do not appear within FPD's records, and we learned of many uses of force that were never officially reported or investigated from reviewing emails between FPD supervisors. Finally, FPD's force files reflect an overrepresentation of ECW uses—a type of force that creates a physical record (a spent ECW cartridge with discharged confetti) and that requires a separate form be filled out. It is much easier for officers to use physical blows and baton strikes without documenting them. Thus, the evidence indicates that a significant amount of force goes unreported within FPD. This in turn raises the possibility that the pattern of unreasonable force is even greater than we found.

Even when force is reported, the force review process falls so short of FPD's policy requirements that it is ineffective at improving officer safety or ensuring that force is used properly. First, and most significantly, supervisors almost never actually investigate force incidents. In almost every case, supervisors appear to view force investigations as a ministerial task, merely summarizing the involved officers' version of events and sometimes relying on the officers' offense report alone. The supervisory review starts and ends with the presumption that the officer's version of events is truthful and that the force was reasonable. As a consequence, though contrary to policy, supervisors almost never interview non-police witnesses, such as the arrestee or any independent witnesses. They do not review critical evidence even when it is readily available. For example, a significant portion of the documented uses of force occurs at the Ferguson jail, which employs surveillance cameras to monitor the area. Yet FPD records provide no indication that a supervisor has ever sought to review the footage for a jail incident. Nor do supervisors examine ECW camera video, even though it is available in FPD's newer model ECWs. Sometimes, supervisors provide no remarks on the use-of-force report, indicating simply, "see offense report."

Our review found the record to be replete with examples of this lack of meaningful supervisory review of force. For example, the use-of-force report for a May 2013 incident states that a suspect claims he had an ECW deployed against him and that he was punched in the head and face. The supervisor concludes simply, "other than the drive stun, no use of force was performed by the officers." The report does not clarify what investigation the supervisor did, if any, to assess the suspect's allegations, or how he determined that the allegations were false. Supervisors also fail to provide recommendations for how to ensure officer safety and minimize the need for force going forward. In January 2014, for instance, a correctional officer used force to subdue an inmate who tried to escape while the correctional officer was moving the inmate's cellmate to another cell without assistance. The supervisor missed the opportunity to recommend that correctional officers not act alone in such risky situations.

Second, supervisors either do not understand or choose not to follow FPD's use-of-force policy. As discussed above, in many of the force incidents we reviewed, it is clear from the officers' offense reports that the force used was, at the very least, contrary to FPD policy. Nonetheless, based on records provided by FPD, it appears that first-line supervisors and the command staff found all but one of the 151 incidents we reviewed to be within policy. This includes the instances of unreasonable ECW use discussed above. FPD policy advises that ECWs are to be used to "overcome active aggression or overt actions of assault." FPD General Order 499.00. They are to be used to "avert[] a potentially injurious or dangerous situation," and never "punitively or for purposes of coercion." FPD General Order 499.04. Simply referring back to these policies should have made clear to supervisors that the many uses of ECWs against subjects who were merely argumentative or passively resistant violated policy.

For example, in April 2014, an intoxicated jail detainee climbed up on the bars in his cell and refused to get down when ordered to by the arresting officer and the correctional officer on duty. The correctional officer then fired an ECW at him, from outside the closed cell door, striking the detainee in the chest and causing him to fall to the ground. In addition to being excessive, this force violated explicit FPD policy that "[p]roper consideration and care should be taken when deploying the X26 TASER on subjects who are in an elevated position or in other circumstance where a fall may cause substantial injury or death." FPD General Order 499.04. The reviewing supervisor deemed the use of force within policy.

Supervisors seem to believe that any level of resistance justifies any level of force. They routinely rely on boilerplate language, such as the statement that the subject took "a fighting stance," to justify force. Such language is not specific enough to understand the specific behavior the officer encountered and thus to determine whether the officer's response was reasonable. Indeed, a report from September 2010 shows how such terms may obscure what happened. In that case, the supervisor wrote that the subject "turned to [the officer] in a fighting stance" even though the officer's report makes clear that he chased and tackled the subject as the subject fled. That particular use of force may have been reasonable, but the use-of-force report reveals how little attention supervisors give to their force investigations. Another common justification, frequently offered by officers who use ECWs to subdue individuals who do not readily put their hands behind their back after being put on the ground, is to claim that a subject's hands were near his waist, where he might have a weapon. Supervisors tend to accept this justification without question.

Third, the review process breaks down even further when officers at the sergeant level or above use force. Instead of reporting their use of force to an official higher up the chain, who could evaluate it objectively, they complete the use-of-force investigation themselves. We found several examples of supervisors investigating their own conduct. When force investigations are conducted by the very officers involved in the incidents, the department is less likely to identify policy and constitutional violations, and the public is less likely to trust the department's commitment to policing itself.

Fourth, the failure of supervisors to investigate and the absence of analysis from their use-of-force reports frustrate review up the chain of command. Lieutenants, the assigned captain, and the Police Chief typically receive at most a one- or two-paragraph summary from supervisors; no witness statements, photographs, or video footage that should have been obtained during the investigation is included. These reviewers are left to rely only on the offense report and the sergeant's cursory summary. To take one example, 21 officers responded to a fight at the high school in March 2013, and several of them used force to take students into custody. FPD records contain only one offense report, which does not describe the actions of all officers who used force. The use-of-force report identifies the involved officers as "multiple" (without names) and provides only a one-paragraph summary stating that students "were grabbed, handcuffed, and restrained using various techniques of control." The offense report reflects that officers collected video from the school's security cameras, but the supervisor apparently never reviewed it. Further, while the offense report contains witness statements, those statements relate to the underlying fight, not the officer use of force, and there appear to be no statements from any of the 21 officers who responded to the fight. It is not possible for higher-level supervisors to adequately assess uses of force with so little information.

In fact, although a use-of-force packet is supposed to include all related documents, in practice only the two-page use-of-force report, that is, the supervisor's brief summary of the incident, goes to the Chief. In the example from the high school, then, the Chief would have known only that there was a fight at the school and that force was used—not which officers used force, what type of force was used, or what the students did to warrant the use of force. Offense reports are available in FPD's records management system, but Chief Jackson told us he rarely retrieves them when reviewing uses of force. The Chief also told us that he has never overturned a supervisor's determination of whether a use of force fell within FPD policy.

Finally, FPD does not perform any comprehensive review of force incidents sufficient to detect patterns of misconduct by a particular officer or unit, or patterns regarding a particular type of force. Indeed, FPD does not keep records in a manner that would allow for such a review. Within FPD's paper storage system, the two-page use-of-force reports (which are usually handwritten) are kept separately from all other documentation, including ECW and pursuit forms for the same incidents. Offense reports are attached to some use-of-force reports but not others. Some use-of-force reports have been removed from FPD's set of force files because the incidents became the subjects of an internal investigation or a lawsuit. As a consequence, when FPD provided us what it considers to be its force files—which, as described above, we have reason to believe do not capture all actual force incidents—a majority of those files were missing a critical document, such as an offense report, ECW report, or the use-of-force report itself. We had to make repeated requests for documents to construct force files amenable to fair review. There were some documents that FPD was unable to locate, even after repeated requests.

With its records incomplete and scattered, the department is unable to implement an early intervention system to identify officers who tend to use excessive force or the need for more training or better equipment—goals explicitly set out by FPD policy. It appears that no annual review of force incidents is conducted, as required by FPD General Order 410.07; indeed, a meaningful annual audit would be impossible. These recordkeeping problems also explain why Chief Jackson told us he could not remember ever imposing discipline for an improper use of force or ordering further training based on force problems.

These deficiencies in use-of-force review can have serious consequences. They make it less likely that officers will be held accountable for excessive force and more likely that constitutional violations will occur. They create potentially devastating liability for the City for failing to put in place systems to ensure officers operate within the bounds of the law. And they result in a police department that does not give its officers the supervision they need to do their jobs safely, effectively, and constitutionally.

B. Ferguson's Municipal Court Practices

The Ferguson municipal court handles most charges brought by FPD, and does so not with the primary goal of administering justice or protecting the rights of the accused, but of maximizing revenue. The impact that revenue concerns have on court operations undermines the court's role as a fair and impartial judicial body.[20] Our investigation has uncovered substantial evidence that the court's procedures are constitutionally deficient and function to impede a person's ability to challenge or resolve a municipal charge, resulting in unnecessarily prolonged cases and an increased likelihood of running afoul of court requirements. At the same time, the court imposes severe penalties when a defendant fails to meet court requirements, including added fines and fees and arrest warrants that are unnecessary and run counter to public safety. These practices both reflect and reinforce an approach to law enforcement in Ferguson that violates the Constitution and undermines police legitimacy and community trust.

Ferguson's municipal court practices combine to cause significant harm to many individuals who have cases pending before the court. Our investigation has found overwhelming evidence of minor municipal code violations resulting in multiple arrests, jail time, and payments that exceed the cost of the original ticket many times over. One woman, discussed above, received two parking tickets for a single violation in 2007 that then totaled $151 plus fees. Over seven years later, she still owed Ferguson $541—after already paying $550 in fines and fees, having multiple arrest warrants issued against her, and being arrested and jailed on several occasions. Another woman told us that when she went to court to try to pay $100 on a $600 outstanding balance, the Court Clerk refused to take the partial payment, even though the woman explained that she was a single mother and could not afford to pay more that month. A 90-year-old man had a warrant issued for his arrest after he failed to timely pay the five citations FPD issued to him during a single traffic stop in 2013. An 83-year-old man had a warrant issued against him when he failed to timely resolve his Derelict Auto violation. A 67-year-old woman told us she was stopped and arrested by a Ferguson police officer for an outstanding warrant for failure to pay a trash-removal citation. She did not know about the warrant until her arrest, and the court ultimately charged her $1,000 in fines, which she continues to pay off in $100 monthly increments despite being on a limited, fixed income. We have heard similar stories from dozens of other individuals and have reviewed court records documenting many additional instances of similarly harsh penalties, often for relatively minor violations.

Our review of police and court records suggests that much of the harm of Ferguson's law enforcement practices in recent years is attributable to the court's routine use of arrest warrants to secure collection and compliance when a person misses a required court appearance or payment. In a case involving a moving violation, procedural failures also result in the suspension of the defendant's license. And, until recently, the court regularly imposed a separate Failure to Appear charge for missed appearances and payments; that charge resulted in an additional fine in the amount of $75.50, plus $26.50 in court costs. *See* Ferguson Mun. Code § 13-58 (repealed Sept. 23, 2014). During the last three years, the court imposed roughly one Failure to Appear charge per every two citations or summonses issued by FPD. Since at least 2010, the court has collected more revenue for Failure to Appear charges than for any other charge. This includes $442,901 in fines for Failure to Appear violations in 2013, which comprised 24% of the total revenue the court collected that year. While the City Council repealed the Failure to Appear ordinance in September 2014, many people continue to owe fines and fees stemming from that charge. And the court continues to issue arrest warrants in every case where that charge previously would have been applied. License suspension practices are similarly unchanged. Once issued, arrest warrants can, and frequently do, lead to arrest and time in jail, despite the fact that the underlying offense did not result in a penalty of imprisonment.[21]

Thus, while the municipal court does not generally deem the code violations that come before it as jail-worthy, it routinely views the failure to appear in court to remit payment to the City as jail-worthy, and commonly issues warrants to arrest individuals who have failed to make timely payment. Similarly, while the municipal court does not have any authority to impose a fine of over $1,000 for any offense, it is not uncommon for individuals to pay more than this amount to the City of Ferguson—in forfeited bond payments, additional Failure to Appear charges, and added court fees—for what may have begun as a simple code violation. In this way, the penalties that the court imposes are driven not by public safety needs, but by financial interests. And despite the harm imposed by these needless penalties, until recently, the City and court did little to respond to the increasing frequency of Failure to Appear charges, and in many respects made court practices more opaque and difficult to navigate.

1. COURT PRACTICES IMPOSE SUBSTANTIAL AND UNNECESSARY BARRIERS TO THE CHALLENGE OR RESOLUTION OF MUNICIPAL CODE VIOLATIONS

It is a hallmark of due process that individuals are entitled to adequate notice of the allegations made against them and to a meaningful opportunity to be heard. *See Cole v. Arkansas*, 333 U.S. 196, 201 (1948); *see also Ward v. Vill. of Monroeville*, 409 U.S. 57, 58–62 (1972) (applying due process requirements to case adjudicated by municipal traffic court). As documented below, however, Ferguson municipal court rules and procedures often fail to provide these basic protections, imposing unnecessary barriers to resolving a citation or summons and thus increasing the likelihood of incurring the severe penalties that result if a code violation is not quickly resolved.

We have concerns not only about the obstacles to resolving a charge even when an individual chooses not to contest it, but also about the trial processes that apply in the rare occasion that a person does attempt to challenge a charge. While it is "axiomatic that a fair trial in a fair tribunal is a basic requirement of due process," *Caperton v. A.T. Massey Coal Co., Inc.*, 556 U.S. 868, 876 (2009), the adjudicative tribunal provided by the Ferguson municipal court appears deficient in many respects.[22] Attempts to raise legal claims are met with retaliatory conduct. In an August 2012 email exchange, for instance, the Court Clerk asked what the Prosecuting Attorney does when an attorney appears in a red light camera case, and the Prosecuting Attorney responded: "I usually dismiss them if the attorney merely requests a recommendation. If the attorney goes off on all of the constitutional stuff, then I tell the attorney to come . . . and argue in front [of] the judge—after that, his client can pay the ticket." We have found evidence of similar adverse action taken against litigants attempting to fulsomely argue a case at trial. The man discussed above who was cited after allowing his child to urinate in a bush attempted to challenge his charges. The man retained counsel who, during trial, was repeatedly interrupted by the court during his cross-examination of the officer. When the attorney objected to the interruptions, the judge told him that, if he continued on this path, "I will hold you in contempt and I will incarcerate you," which, as discussed below, the court has done in the past to others appearing before it. The attorney told us that, believing no line of questioning would alter the outcome, he tempered his defense so as not to be jailed. Notably, at that trial, even though the testifying officer had previously been found untruthful during an official FPD investigation, the prosecuting attorney presented his testimony without informing defendant of that fact, and the court credited that testimony.[23] The evidence thus suggests substantial deficiencies in the manner in which the court conducts trials.

Even where defendants opt not to challenge their charges, a number of court processes make resolving a case exceedingly difficult. City officials and FPD officers we spoke with nearly uniformly asserted that individuals' experiences when they become embroiled in Ferguson's municipal code enforcement are due not to any failings in Ferguson's law enforcement practices, but rather to those individuals' lack of "personal responsibility." But these statements ignore the barriers to resolving a case that court practices impose, including: 1) a lack of transparency regarding rights and responsibilities; 2) requiring in-person appearance to resolve most municipal charges; 3) policies that exacerbate the harms of Missouri's law requiring license suspension where a person fails to appear on a moving violation charge; 4) basic access deficiencies that frustrate a person's ability to resolve even those charges that do not require in-court appearance; and 5) legally inadequate fine assessment methods that do not appropriately consider a person's ability to pay and do not provide alternatives to fines for those living in or near poverty. Together, these barriers impose considerable hardship. We have heard repeated reports, and found evidence in court records, of people appearing in court many times—in some instances on more than ten occasions—to try to resolve a case but being unable to do so, and subsequently having additional fines, fees, and arrest warrants issued against them.

a. Court Practices and Procedural Deficiencies Create a Lack of Transparency Regarding Rights and Responsibilities

It is often difficult for an individual who receives a municipal citation or summons in Ferguson to know how much is owed, where and how to pay the ticket, what the options for payment are, what rights the individual has, and what the consequences are for various actions or oversights. The initial information provided to people who are cited for violating Ferguson's municipal code is often incomplete or inconsistent. Communication with municipal court defendants is haphazard and known by the court to be unreliable. And the court's procedures and operations are ambiguous, are not written down, and are not transparent or even available to the public on the court's website or elsewhere.

The rules and procedures of the court are difficult for the public to discern. Aside from a small number of exceptions, the Municipal Judge issues rules of practice and procedure verbally and on an ad hoc basis. Until recently, on the rare occasion that the Judge issued a written order that altered court practices, those orders were not distributed broadly to court and other FPD officials whose actions they affect and were not readily accessible to the public. Further, Ferguson, unlike other courts in the region, does not include any information about its operations on its website other than inaccurate instructions about how to make payment.[24] Court staff acknowledged during our investigation that the public would benefit from increased information about how to resolve cases and about court practices and procedures. Yet neither the court nor other City officials have undertaken efforts to make court operations more transparent in order to ensure that litigants understand their rights or court procedures, or to enable the public to assess whether the court is operating in a fair manner.

Current court practices fail to provide adequate information even to those who are charged with a municipal violation. The lack of clarity about a person's rights and responsibilities often begins from the moment a person is issued a citation. For some offenses, FPD uses state of Missouri uniform citations, and typically indicates on the ticket the assigned court date for the offense. Many times, however, FPD officers omit critical information from the citation, which makes it impossible for a person to determine the specific nature of the offense charged, the amount of the fine owed, or whether a court appearance is required or some alternative method of payment is available. In some cases, citations fail to indicate the offense charged altogether; in November 2013, for instance, court staff wrote FPD patrol to "see what [a] ticket was for" because it "does not have a charge on it." In other cases, a ticket will indicate a charge but omit other crucial information. For example, speeding tickets often fail to indicate the alleged speed observed, even though both the fine owed and whether a court appearance is mandatory depends upon the specific speed alleged. Evidence shows that in some of these cases, a person has appeared in court but been unable to resolve the citation because of the missing information. In June 2014, for instance, a court clerk wrote to an FPD officer: "The above ticket . . . does not have a speed in it. The guy came in and we had to send him away. Can you email me the speed when you get time." Separate and apart from the difficulties these omissions create for people, the fact that the court staff routinely add the speed to tickets weeks after they are issued raises concerns about the accuracy and reliability of officers' assertions in official records.

We have also found evidence that in issuing citations, FPD officers frequently provide people with incorrect information about the date and time of their assigned court session. In November 2012, court staff emailed the two patrol lieutenants asking: "Would you please be so kind to tell your squads to check their ct. dates and times. We are getting quite a few wrong dates and times [on tickets]." In December 2012, a court clerk emailed an FPD officer to inform him that while he had been putting 6:00 p.m. on his citations that month, the scheduled court session was actually a morning session. More recently, in March 2014, an officer wrote a court clerk because the officer had issued a citation that listed the court date as ten days later than the actual court date assigned. Some of these emails indicate that court staff planned to send a letter to the person who was cited. As noted below, however, such letters often are returned to the court as undeliverable. It is thus unsurprising that, on one occasion, a City employee who works in the building where court was held wrote the Court Clerk to tell her that "[a] few people stopped by tonight looking for court and I referred them to you." The email notes that one person insisted on providing her information so the employee could "vouch for her appearance for Night Court." The email does not identify any other individual who showed up for court that night, nor does it state that any steps were taken to ensure that those assigned the incorrect court date did not have Failure to Appear charges and fines imposed, arrest warrants issued against them, or their licenses suspended.

Even if the citation a person receives has been properly filled out, it is often unclear whether a court appearance is required or if some other method of resolving a case is available. Ferguson has a schedule that establishes fixed fines for a limited number of violations that do not require court appearance. Nonetheless, this list—called the "TVB" or "Traffic Violations Bureau" list—is incomplete and does not provide sufficient clarity regarding whether a court appearance is mandatory. Court staff members have themselves informed us that there are certain offenses for which they will sometimes require a court appearance and other times not, depending on their own assessment of whether an appearance should be required in a given case. That information, however, is not reliably communicated to the person who has been given the citation.

Although the City of Ferguson frequently bears responsibility for giving people misinformation about when they must appear in court, Ferguson does little to ensure that persons who have missed a court date are properly notified of the consequences that result from an additional missed appearance, such as arrest or losing their driver's licenses, or that those consequences have already been levied. If a person misses a required appearance, it is the purported practice of court staff to send a letter that sets a new court date and informs the defendant that missing the next appearance will result in an arrest warrant being issued. But court staff do not even claim

to send these letters before issuing warrants if an individual is on a payment plan and misses a payment, or if a person already has an outstanding
warrant on a different offense; in those cases, the court issues a warrant
after a single missed payment or appearance. Further, even for the cases
in which the court says it does send such letters prior to issuing a warrant,
court records suggest that those letters are often not actually sent. Even
where a letter is sent, some are returned to court, and court staff told us
that in those cases, they make no additional effort to notify the individual
of the new court date or the consequences of non-appearance. Court staff
and staff from other municipal courts have informed us that defendants in
poverty are more likely not to receive such a letter from court because they
frequently change residence.

If an individual misses a second court date, an arrest warrant is issued,
without any confirmation that the individual received notice of that second
court date. In the past, when the court issued a warrant it would also send
notice to the individual that a warrant was issued against them and telling
them to appear at the police department to resolve the matter. This notice
did not provide the basis of the arrest warrant or describe how it might be
resolved. In any case, Ferguson stopped providing even this incomplete
notice in 2012. In explaining the decision to stop sending this warrant notice, the Court Clerk wrote in a June 2011 email to Chief Jackson that "this
will save the cost of warrant cards and postage" and "it is not necessary
to send out these cards." Some court employees, however, told us that the
notice letter had been useful—at least for those who received it—and that
they believe it should still be sent. That the court discontinued what little
notice it was providing to people in advance of issuing a warrant is particularly troubling given that, during our investigation, we spoke with several
individuals who were arrested without ever knowing that a warrant was
outstanding.[25]

Once a warrant is issued, a person can clear the warrant by appearing
at the court window in the police department and paying a pre-determined
bond. However, that process is itself not communicated to the public and, in
any case, is only useful if an individual knows there is a warrant for her or

his arrest. Court clerks told us that in some cases they deem sympathetic in their own discretion, they will cancel the warrant without a bond. Further, it appears that if a person is aware of an outstanding warrant but believes that the warrant was issued in error, that person can petition the Municipal Judge to cancel the warrant only after the bond is paid in full. If a person cannot afford to pay the bond, there is no opportunity to seek recourse from the court.

If a person is arrested on an outstanding warrant—or as the result of an encounter with FPD—it is often difficult to secure release with a bond payment, not only because of the inordinately high bond amounts discussed below, but also because of procedural obstacles. In practice, bond procedures depart from those articulated in official policy, and are arbitrary and confusing. FPD staff have told us that correctional officers have at times tried to find a warrant in the court's files to determine the bond amount owed, but have been unable to do so. This is unsurprising given the existence of what has been described to us as "drawers and drawers of warrants." In some cases, people have attempted to pay a bond to secure the release of a family member in FPD custody, but were not even seen by FPD staff. On one occasion, an FPD staff member reported to an FPD captain that a person "came to the station last night and waited to post bond for [a detainee], from 1:00 until 3:30. No one ever came up to get her money and no one informed her that she was going to have to wait that long."

b. Needlessly Requiring In-Court Appearances for Most Code Violations Imposes Unnecessary Obstacles to Resolving Cases

Ferguson requires far more defendants to appear in court than is required under state law. Under Missouri Supreme Court rules, there is a short list of violations that require the violator's appearance in court: any violation resulting in personal injury or property damage; driving while intoxicated; driving without a proper license; and attempting to elude a police officer. *See* Mo. Sup. Ct. R. 37.49. The municipal judge of each court has the discretion to expand this list of "must appears," and Ferguson's municipal court has expanded it exponentially: of 376 actively charged municipal offenses, court staff informed us that approximately 229 typically require an appearance in court before the fine can be paid, including Dog Creating Nuisance, Equipment Violations, No Passing Zone, Housing – Overgrown Vegetation, and Failure to Remove Leaf Debris. Ferguson requires these court appearances regardless of whether the individual is contesting the charges.

Requiring an individual to appear at a specific place and time to pay a citation makes it far more likely that the individual will fail to appear or pay the citation on time, quickly resulting, in Ferguson, in an arrest warrant and a suspended license. Even setting aside the fact that people often receive inaccurate information about when they must appear in court, the in-person appearance requirement imposes particular difficulties on low-wage workers, single parents, and those with limited access to reliable transportation. Requiring an individual to appear in court also imposes particular burdens on those with jobs that have set hours that may conflict with an assigned court session. Court sessions are sometimes set during the workday and sometimes in the early evening. Additionally, while court dates can be set for several months after the citation was issued, in some cases they can also be issued as early as a week after a citation is received. For example, court staff have instructed FPD officers that derelict auto violations must be set for the "very next court date even if it is just a week . . . or so away." This can add an additional obstacle for those with firmly established employment schedules.

There are also historical reasons, of which the City is well-aware, that many Ferguson residents may not appear in court. Some individuals fear that if they cannot immediately pay the fines they owe, they will be arrested and sent to jail. Ferguson court staff members told us that they believe the high number of missed court appearances in their court is attributable, in part, to this popular belief. These fears are well founded. While Judge Brockmeyer has told us that he has never sentenced someone to jail time for being unable to pay a fine, we have found evidence that the Judge has held people appearing in court for contempt on account of their unwillingness to answer questions and sentenced those individuals to jail time. In December 2013, the FPD officer assigned to provide security at a court session directly emailed the City Manager to provide notice that "Judge Brock-meyer ordered [a defendant] arrested tonight after [he] refused to answer any questions and told the Judge that he had no jurisdiction. This happened on two separate occasions and with the second occasion when [the defendant] continued with his refusal to answer the Judge, he was order[ed] to be arrested and held for 10 days."[26] We also spoke with a woman who told us that, after asking questions in court, FPD officers arrested her for Contempt of Court at the instructions of the Court Clerk. Moreover, we have also received a report of an FPD officer arresting an individual at court for an outstanding warrant. In that instance, which occurred in April 2014, the individual—who was in court to make a fine payment—was approached by an FPD officer, asked to step outside of the court session, and was immediately arrested. In addition, as Ferguson's Municipal Judge confirmed, it is not uncommon for him to add charges and assess additional fines when a defendant challenges the citation that brought the defendant into court. Appearing in court in Ferguson also requires waits that can stretch into hours, sometimes outdoors in inclement weather. Many individuals report being treated dismissively, or worse, by court staff and the Municipal Judge.

Further, as Ferguson officials have told us, many people have experience with the numerous other municipal courts in St. Louis County that informs individuals' expectations about the Ferguson municipal court. Our investigation shows that other municipalities in the area have engaged in a number of practices that have the effect of discouraging people from attending court sessions. For instance, court clerks from other municipalities have told us that they have seen judges order people arrested if they appear in court with an outstanding warrant but are unable to pay the fine owed or post the bond amount listed on the warrant. Indeed, one municipal judge from a neighboring municipality told us that this practice has resulted in what he believes to be a widespread belief that those who attend court but cannot pay will be immediately arrested—a view that municipal judge says is "entirely the municipal courts' fault" for perpetuating because they have not taken steps to correct it. Recent reports have documented other problematic practices. For example, a June 2014 letter from Presiding Circuit Court Judge

Maura McShane to municipal court judges in the region discussed troubling and possibly unlawful practices of municipal courts in St. Louis County that served to prevent the public from attending court sessions. These practices included not allowing children in court. Indeed, as late as October 2014, the municipal court website in the neighboring municipality of Bel Ridge—where Judge Brockmeyer serves as prosecutor—stated that children are not allowed in court. While it appears that Ferguson's court has always allowed children, we talked with people who assumed it did not because of their experiences in other courts. One man told us he was aggressively questioned by FPD officers after he left his child outside court with a friend because of this assumption. Thus, even though Ferguson might not engage in some of these practices, and while it may even be the case that other municipalities have themselves implemented reforms, the long history of these practices continues to shape community members' views of what might happen to them if they attend court.

Court officials have told us that Ferguson's expansive list of "must appear" offenses is not driven by any public safety need. That is underscored by the fact that, in some cases, attorneys are allowed to resolve such offenses over the phone without making any appearance in court. Nonetheless, despite the acknowledged obstacles to appearing in person in court and the lack of any articulated need to appear in court in all but a few instances, Ferguson has taken few, if any, steps to reduce the number of cases that require a court appearance.

c. Driver's License Suspensions Mandated by State Law and Unnecessarily Prolonged by Ferguson Make It Difficult to Resolve a Case and Impose Substantial Hardship

For many who have already had a warrant issued against them for failing to either appear or make a required payment, appearing in court is made especially difficult by the fact that their warrants likely resulted in the suspension of their driver's licenses. Pursuant to Missouri state law, anyone who fails to pay a traffic citation for a moving violation on time, or who fails to appear in court regarding a moving traffic violation, has his or her driver's license suspended. Mo. Rev. Stat. § 302.341.1. Thus, by virtue of having their licenses suspended, those who have already missed a required court appearance are more likely to fail to meet subsequent court obligations if they require physically appearing in court—fostering a cycle of missed appearances that is difficult to end. That is particularly so given what some City officials from Ferguson and surrounding communities have called substandard public transportation options. We spoke with one woman who had her license suspended because she received a Failure to Appear charge in Ferguson and so had to rely on a friend to drive her to court. When her friend canceled, she had no other means of getting to court on time, missed court, and had another Failure to Appear charge and arrest warrant issued against her—adding to the charges that required resolution before her license could be reinstated.[27]

To be clear, responsibility for the hardship imposed by automatically suspending a person's license for failing to appear in a traffic case rests largely with this state law. Notably, however, Ferguson's own discretionary practices amplify and prolong that law's impact. A temporary suspension can be lifted with a compliance letter from the municipal court, but the Ferguson municipal court does not issue compliance letters unless a person has satisfied the *entire fine* pending on the charge that caused the suspension. This rule is not mandated by state law, which instead provides a municipality with the authority to decide when to issue a compliance letter. *See* Mo. Rev. Stat. § 302.341.1 ("Such suspension shall remain in effect until the court with the subject pending charge requests setting aside the noncompliance suspension pending final disposition."). Indeed, Ferguson court staff told us that they will issue compliance letters before full payment has been made for cases that they determine, in their unguided discretion, to be sympathetic.

This rule and the Ferguson practices that magnify its impact underscore how missed court appearances can have broad ramifications for individuals' ability to maintain a job and care for their families. We spoke with one woman who received three citations during a single incident in 2013 in which she pulled to the side of the road to allow a police car to pass, was confronted by the officer for doing so, and was cited for obstructing traffic, failing to signal, and not wearing a seatbelt. The woman appeared in court to challenge those citations, was told a new trial date would be mailed to her, and instead received notice from the Missouri Department of Revenue several months later that her license was suspended. Upon informing the Court Clerk that she never received notice of her court date, the Clerk told her the trial date had passed two weeks earlier and that there was now a warrant for her arrest pending.[28] Given that the woman's license was suspended only two weeks after her trial date, it appears the court did not send a warning letter before entering a warrant and suspending the license, contrary to purported policy. Court records likewise do not indicate a letter being sent. The woman asked to see the Municipal Judge to explain the situation, but court staff informed her that she could only see the Judge if she was issued a new court date and that she would only be issued a new court date if she paid her $200 bond. With no opportunity to further petition the court, she wrote to Mayor Knowles about her situation, stating:

> Although I feel I have been harassed, wronged and unjustly done by Ferguson . . . [w]hat I am upset and concerned about is my driver's license being suspended. I was told that I may not be able to [be] reinstate[d] until the tickets are taken care of. I am a hard working mother of two children and I cannot by any means take care of my family or work with my license being suspended and being unable to drive. I have to have [a] valid license to keep my job because I transport clients that I work with not to mention I drive my children back and forth to school, practices and rehearsals on a daily basis. I am writing this letter because no one has been able to help me and I am really hoping that I can get some help getting this issue resolved expediently.

It appears that, at the Mayor's request, the court entered "Not Guilty" dispositions on her cases, several months after they first resulted in the license suspension.

d. Court Operations Impose Obstacles to Resolving Even Those Offenses that Do Not Require In-Person Court Appearance

The limited number of code violations that do not require an in-person court appearance can likewise be difficult to resolve, even if a person can afford to do so. The court has accepted mailed payments for some time and has recently begun to accept online payments, but the court's website suggests that in-person payment is required and provides no information that payment online or by mail is an option. As a result, many people try to remit payment to the court window within the police department. But community members have informed us that the court window often closes earlier than the posted hours indicate. Indeed, during our investigation, we observed the court window close at 4:30 p.m. on days where an evening court session was not being held, despite the fact that both the Ferguson City website and the Missouri Courts website state that the window closes at 5:00 p.m.[29] On one such occasion, we observed two different sets of people arrive after 4:30 p.m. but before 5:00 p.m. One man told us his ticket payment was due that day. Another woman arrived in the rain with her small child, unsuccessfully attempted to call someone to the window, and left. Even when the court window is technically open, we have seen people standing at the window waiting for a response to their knocks for long periods of time, sometimes in inclement weather—even as court staff sat inside the police department tending to their normal duties.

As noted above, documents we reviewed showed that even where individuals are successful in talking with court staff about a citation, FPD-issued citations are sometimes so deficient that court staff are unable to determine what the fine, or even charge, is supposed to be. Evidence also shows that court staff have at times been unable to even find a person's case file, often because the FPD officer who issued the ticket failed to properly file a copy. In these cases, a person is left unable to resolve her or his citation.

e. High Fines, Coupled with Legally Inadequate Ability-to-Pay Determinations and Insufficient Alternatives to Immediate Payment, Impose a Significant Burden on People Living In or Near Poverty

It is common for a single traffic stop or other encounter with FPD to give rise to fines in amounts that a person living in poverty is unable to immediately pay. This fact is attributable in part to FPD's practice of issuing multiple citations—frequently three or more—on a single stop. This fact is also attributable to the fine assessment practices of the Ferguson municipal court, including not only the high fine amounts imposed, but also the inadequate process available for those who cannot afford to pay a fine. Even setting aside cases where additional fines and fees were imposed for Failure to Appear violations, our investigation found instances in which the court charged $302 for a single Manner of Walking violation; $427 for a single Peace Disturbance violation; $531 for High Grass and Weeds; $777 for Resisting Arrest; and $792 for Failure to Obey, and $527 for Failure to Comply, which officers appear to use interchangeably.

For many, the hardship of the fine amounts imposed is exacerbated by the fact that they owe similar fines in other, neighboring municipalities. We spoke with one woman who, in addition to owing several hundred dollars in fines to Ferguson, also owed fines to the municipal courts in Jennings and Edmundson. In total, she owed over $2,500 in fines and fees, even after already making over $1,000 in payments and clearing cases in several other municipalities. This woman's case is not unique. We have heard reports from many individuals and even City officials that, in light of the large number of municipalities in the area immediately surrounding Ferguson, most of which have their own police departments and municipal courts, it is common for people to face significant fines from many municipalities.

City officials have extolled that the Ferguson preset fine schedule establishes fines that are "at or near the top of the list" compared with other municipalities across a large number of offenses. A more recent comparison of the preset fines of roughly 70 municipal courts in the region confirms that Ferguson's fine amounts are above regional averages for many offenses, particularly discretionary offenses such as non-speeding-related traffic offenses. That comparison also shows that Ferguson imposes the highest fine of any of those roughly 70 municipalities for the offense of Failing to Provide Proof of Insurance; Ferguson charges $375, whereas the average fine imposed is $186 and the median fine imposed is $175. In 2013 alone, the Ferguson court collected over $286,000 in fines for that offense—more than any other offense except Failure to Appear.

The fines that the court imposes for offenses without preset fines are more difficult to evaluate precisely because they are imposed on a case-by-case basis. Typically, however, in imposing fines for non-TVB offenses during court sessions, the Municipal Judge adopts the fine recommendations of the Prosecuting Attorney—who also serves as the Ferguson City Attorney. As discussed above, court staff have communicated with the Municipal Judge regarding the need to ensure that the prosecutor's recommended fines are sufficiently high because "[w]e need to keep up our revenue." We were also told of at least one incident in which an attorney received a fine recommendation from the prosecutor for his client, but when the client went to court to pay the fine, a clerk refused payment, informing her that there was an additional $100 owed beyond the fine recommended by the prosecutor.

The court imposes these fines without providing any process by which a person can seek a fine reduction on account of financial incapacity. The court does not provide any opportunity for a person unable to pay a preset TVB fine to seek a modification of the fine amount. Nor does the court consider a person's financial ability to pay in determining how much of a fine to impose in cases without preset fines. The Ferguson court's failure to assess a defendant's ability to pay stands in direct tension with Missouri law, which instructs that in determining the amount and the method of payment of a fine, a court "shall, insofar as practicable, proportion the fine to the burden that payment will impose in view of the financial resources of an individual." Mo. Rev. Stat. § 560.026.

In lieu of proportioning a fine to a particular individual's ability to pay or allowing a process by which a person could petition the court for a reduction, the court offers payment plans to those who cannot afford to immediately pay in full. But such payment plans do not serve as a substitute for an ability-to-pay determination, which, properly employed, can enable a person in some cases to pay in full and resolve the case. Moreover, the court's rules regarding payment plans are themselves severe. Unlike some other municipalities that require a $50 monthly payment, Ferguson's standard payment plan requires payments of $100 per month, which remains a difficult amount for many to pay, especially those who are also making payments to other municipalities. Further, the court treats a single missed, partial, or untimely payment as a missed appearance. In such a case, the court immediately issues an arrest warrant without any notice or opportunity to explain why a payment was missed—for example, because the person was sick, or the court closed its doors early that day. The court reportedly has softened this rule during the course of our investigation by allowing a person who has missed a payment to go to court to seek leave for not paying the full amount owed. However, even this softened rule provides minimal relief, as making this request requires a person to appear in court the first Wednesday of the month at 11:00 a.m. If a person misses that session, the court immediately issues an arrest warrant.

Before the court provided this Wednesday morning court session for those on payment plans, court staff frequently rejected requests from payment plan participants to reduce or continue monthly payments—leaving individuals unable to make the required payment with no recourse besides incurring a Failure to Appear charge, receiving additional fines, and having an arrest warrant issued. In July 2014, an assistant court clerk wrote in an email that she rejected a defendant's request for a reduced monthly payment on account of inability to pay and told the defendant, "everyone says [they] can't pay." This is consistent with earlier noted statements by the acting Ferguson prosecutor that he stopped granting "needless requests for continuances from the payment docket." Another defendant who owed $1,002 in fines and fees stemming from a Driving with a Revoked License charge wrote to a City official that he would be unable to make his required monthly payment but hoped to avoid having a warrant issued. He explained that he was unemployed, that the court had put him on a payment plan only a week before his first payment was due, and that he did not have enough time to gather enough money. He implored the City to provide "some kind of community service to work off the fines/fees," stating that "I want to pay you guys what I owe" and "I have been trying to scrape up what I can," but that "with warrants it's hard to get a job." The City official forwarded the request to a court clerk, who noted that the underlying charge dated back to 2007, that five Failure to Appear charges had been levied, and that no payments had yet been made. The clerk responded: "In this certain case [the defendant] will go to warrant." Records show that, only a week earlier, this same clerk asked a court clerk from another municipality to clear a ticket for former Ferguson Police Chief Moonier as a "courtesy." And, only a month later, that same clerk also helped the Ferguson Collector of Revenue clear two citations issued by neighboring municipalities.

Ferguson does not typically offer community service as an alternative to fines. City officials have emphasized to us that Ferguson is one of only a few municipalities in the region to provide any form of a community service program, and that the program that is available is well run. But the program, which began in February 2014, is only available on a limited basis, mostly to certain defendants who are 19 years old or younger.[30] We have heard directly from individuals who could not afford to pay their fines—and thus accumulated additional charges and fines and had warrants issued against them—that they requested a community service alternative to monetary payment but were told no such alternative existed. One man who still owes $1,100 stemming from a speeding and seatbelt violation from 2000 told us that he has been arrested repeatedly in connection with the fines he cannot afford to pay, and that "no one is willing to work with him to find an alternative solution." City officials have recognized the need to provide a meaningful community service option. In August 2013, one City Councilmember wrote to the City Manager and the Mayor that, "[f]or a few years now we have talked about offering community service to those who can't afford to pay their fines, but we haven't actually made it happen." The Councilmember noted the benefits of such a program, including that it would "keep those people that simply don't have the money to pay their fines from constantly being arrested and going to jail, only to be released and do it all over again."

2. THE COURT IMPOSES UNDULY HARSH PENALTIES FOR MISSED PAYMENTS OR APPEARANCES

The procedural deficiencies identified above work together to make it exceedingly difficult to resolve a case and exceedingly easy to run afoul of the court's stringent and confusing rules, particularly for those living in or near poverty. That the court is at least in part responsible for causing cases to protract and result in technical violations has not prevented it from imposing significant penalties when those violations occur. Although Ferguson's court—unlike many other municipal courts in the region—has ceased imposing the Failure to Appear charge, the court continues to routinely issue arrest warrants for missed appearances and missed payments. The evidence we have found shows that these arrest warrants are used almost exclusively for the purpose of compelling payment through the threat of incarceration. The evidence also shows that the harms of the court's warrant practices are exacerbated by the court's bond procedures, which impose unnecessary obstacles to clearing a warrant or securing release after being arrested on a warrant and often function to further prolong a case and a person's involvement in the municipal justice system. These practices—together with the consequences to individuals and communities that result—raise significant due process and equal protection concerns.

a. The Ferguson Municipal Court Uses Arrest Warrants Primarily as a Means of Securing Payment

Ferguson's municipal court issues arrest warrants at a rate that police officials have called, in internal emails, "staggering." According to the court's own figures, as of December 2014, over 16,000 people had outstanding arrest warrants that had been issued by the court. In fiscal year 2013 alone, the court issued warrants to approximately 9,007 people. Many of those individuals had warrants issued on multiple charges, as the 9,007 warrants applied to 32,975 different offenses.

In the wake of several news accounts indicating that the Ferguson municipal court issued over 32,000 warrants in fiscal year 2013, court staff determined that it had mistakenly reported to the state of Missouri the number of charged offenses that had warrants (32,975), not the number of people who had warrants outstanding (9,007). Our investigation indicates that is the case. In any event, it is probative of FPD's enforcement practices that those roughly 9,000 warrants were issued for over 32,000 offenses. Moreover, for those against whom a warrant is issued, the number of offenses included within the warrant has tremendous practical importance. As discussed below, the bond amount a person must pay to clear a warrant before an arrest occurs, or to secure release once a warrant has been executed, is often dependent on the number of offenses to which the warrant applies. And, that the court issued warrants for the arrest of roughly 9,000 people is itself not insignificant; even under that calculation, Ferguson has one of the highest warrant totals in the region.

The large number of warrants issued by the court, by any count, is due exclusively to the fact that the court uses arrest warrants and the threat of arrest as its primary tool for collecting outstanding fines for municipal code violations. With extremely limited exceptions, every warrant issued by the Ferguson municipal court was issued because: 1) a person missed consecutive court appearances, or 2) a person missed a single required fine payment as part of a payment plan. Under current court policy, the court issues a warrant in every case where either of those circumstances arises—regardless of the severity of the code violation that the case involves. Indeed, the court rarely issues a warrant for any other purpose. FPD does not request arrest or any other kind of warrants from the Ferguson municipal court; in fact, FPD officers told us that they have been instructed not to file warrant applications with the municipal court because the court does not have the capacity to consider them.

While issuing municipal warrants against people who have not appeared or paid their municipal code violation fines is sometimes framed as addressing the failure to abide by court rules, in practice, it is clear that warrants are primarily issued to coerce payment.[31] One municipal judge from a neighboring municipality told us that the use of the Failure to Appear charge "provides cushion for judges against the attack that the court is operating as a debtor's prison." And the Municipal Judge in Ferguson has acknowledged repeatedly that the warrants the court issues are not put in place for public safety purposes. Indeed, once a warrant issues, there is no urgency within FPD to actually execute it. Court staff reported that they typically take weeks, if not months, to enter warrants into the system that enables patrol officers to determine if a person they encounter has an outstanding warrant. As of December 2014, for example, some warrants issued in September 2014 were not yet detectable to officers in the field. Court staff also informed us that no one from FPD has ever commented on that lag or prioritized closing it. Nor does there seem to be any public safety obstacle to eliminating failure to appear warrants altogether. The court has, in fact, adopted a temporary "warrant recall program" that allows individuals who show up to court to immediately have their warrants recalled and a new court date assigned. And, under longstanding practice, once an attorney makes an appearance in a case, the court automatically discharges any pending warrants.

That the primary role of warrants is not to protect public safety but rather to facilitate fine collection is further evidenced by the fact that the warrants issued by the court are overwhelmingly issued in non-criminal traffic cases that would not themselves result in a penalty of imprisonment. From 2010 to December 2014, the offenses (besides Failure to Appear ordinance violations) that most often led to a municipal warrant were: Driving While License Is Suspended, Expired License Plates, Failure to Register a Vehicle, No Proof of Insurance, and Speed Limit violations. These offenses comprised the majority of offenses that led to a warrant not because they are more severe than other offenses, but rather because every missed appearance or payment on any charge results in a warrant, and these were some of the most common charges brought by FPD during that period.

Even though these underlying code violations would not on their own result in a penalty of imprisonment, arrest and detention are not uncommon once a warrant enters on a case. We have found that FPD officers frequently check individuals for warrants, even when the person is not reasonably suspected of engaging in any criminal activity, and, if a municipal warrant exists, will often make an arrest. City officials have told us that the decision to arrest a person for an outstanding warrant is "highly discretionary" and that officers will frequently not arrest unless the person is "ignorant." Records show, however, that officers do arrest individuals for outstanding municipal warrants with considerable frequency. Jail records are poorly managed, and data on jail bookings is only available as of April 2014. But during the roughly six-month period from April to September 2014, 256 people were booked into the Ferguson City Jail after being arrested at least in part for an outstanding warrant—96% of whom were African American. Of these individuals, 28 were held for longer than two days, and 27 of these 28 people were black.

Similarly, data collected during vehicle stops shows that, during a larger period of time between October 2012 and October 2014, FPD arrested roughly 460 individuals following a vehicle stop *solely* because they had outstanding warrants. This figure is likely a significant underrepresentation of the total number of people arrested for outstanding warrants during that period, as it does not include those people arrested on outstanding warrants not during traffic stops; nor does it include those people arrested during traffic stops for multiple reasons, but who might not have been stopped, much less arrested, without the officer performing a warrant check on the car and finding an outstanding warrant. Even among this limited pool, the data shows the disparate impact these arrests have on African Americans. Of the 460 individuals arrested during traffic stops solely for outstanding warrants, 443 individuals—or 96%—were African American.

That data also does not include those people arrested by *other* municipal police departments on the basis of an outstanding warrant issued by Ferguson. As has been widely reported in recent months, many municipal police departments in the region identify people with warrants pending in other towns and then arrest and hold those individuals on behalf of those towns. FPD's records show that it routinely arrests individuals on warrants issued by other jurisdictions. And, although we did not review the records of other departments, we have heard reports of many individuals who were arrested for a Ferguson-issued warrant by police officers outside of Ferguson. On some occasions, Ferguson will decline to pick up a person arrested in a different municipality for a Ferguson warrant and, after however long it takes for that decision to be made, the person will be released, sometimes after being required to pay bond. On other occasions, Ferguson will send an officer to retrieve the person for incarceration in the Ferguson City Jail; FPD supervisors have in fact instructed officers to do so "regardless of the charge or the bond amount, or the number of prisoners we have in custody." We found evidence of FPD officers traveling more than 200 miles to retrieve a person detained by another agency on a Ferguson municipal warrant.

Because of the large number of municipalities in the region, many of which have warrant practices similar to Ferguson, it is not unusual for a person to be arrested by one department, have outstanding warrants pending in other police departments, and be handed off from one department to another until all warrants are cleared. We have heard of individuals who have run out of money during this process—referred to by many as the "muni shuffle"—and as a result were detained for a week or longer.

The large number of municipal court warrants being issued, many of which lead to arrest, raises significant due process and equal protection concerns. In particular, Ferguson's practice of automatically treating a missed payment as a failure to appear—thus triggering an arrest warrant and possible incarceration—is directly at odds with well-established law that prohibits "punishing a person for his poverty." *Bearden v. Georgia*, 461 U.S. 660, 671 (1983); *see also Tate v. Short*, 401 U.S. 395, 398 (1971). In *Bearden*, the Supreme Court found unconstitutional a state's decision to revoke probation and sentence a defendant to prison because the defendant was unable to pay a required fine. Bearden, 461 U.S. at 672–73. The Court held that before imposing imprisonment, a court must first inquire as to whether the missed payment was attributable to an inability to pay and, if so, "consider alternate measures of punishment other than imprisonment." *Id.* at 672; *see also Martin v. Solem*, 801 F.2d 324, 332 (8th Cir. 1986) noting that the state court had failed to adequately determine, as required by *Bearden*, whether the defendant had "made sufficient bona fide efforts legally to acquire the resources to pay," but nonetheless denying habeas relief because the defendant's failure to pay was due not to indigency but his "willful refusal to pay").

The Ferguson court, however, has in the past routinely issued arrest warrants when a person is unable to make a required fine payment without any ability-to-pay determination. While the court does not *sentence* a defendant to jail in such a case, the result is often equivalent to what *Bearden* proscribes: the incarceration of a defendant solely because of an inability to pay a fine. In response to concerns about issuing warrants in such cases, Ferguson officials have told us that without issuing warrants and threatening incarceration, they have no ability to secure payment. But the Supreme Court rejected that argument, finding that states are "not powerless to enforce judgments against those financially unable to pay a fine," and noting that—especially in cases like those at issue here in which the court has already made a determination that penological interests do *not* demand incarceration—a court can "establish a reduced fine or alternate public service in lieu of a fine that adequately serves the state's goals of punishment and deterrence, given the defendant's diminished financial resources."[32] *Id.* As discussed above, however, Ferguson has not established any such alternative.[33]

b. Ferguson's Bond Practices Impose Undue Hardship on Those Seeking to Secure Release from the Ferguson City Jail

Our investigation found substantial deficiencies in the way Ferguson police and court officials set, accept, refund, and forfeit bond payments. Recently, in response to concerns raised during our investigation, the City implemented several changes to its bond practices, most of which apply to those detained after a warrantless arrest.[34] These changes represent positive developments, but many deficiencies remain.[35] Given the high number of arrest warrants issued by the municipal court—and given that in many cases a person can only clear a pending warrant or secure release from detention by posting bond—the deficiencies identified below impose significant harm to individuals in Ferguson.

Current bond practices are unclear and inconsistent. Information provided by the City reveals a haphazard bond system that results in people being erroneously arrested, and some people paying bond but not getting credit for having done so. Documents describe officers finding hundred dollar bills in their pockets that were given to them for bond payment and not remembering which jail detainee provided them; bond paperwork being found on the floor; and individuals being arrested after their bonds had been accepted because the corresponding warrants were never cancelled. At one point in 2012, Ferguson's Court Clerk called such issues a "daily problem." The City's practices for receiving and tracking bond payments have not changed appreciably since then.

The practices for setting bond are similarly erratic. The Municipal Judge advised us that he sets all bonds upon issuing an arrest warrant. We found, however, that bond amounts are mostly set by court staff, and are rarely even reviewed by the Judge. While court staff told us that the current bond schedule requires a bond of $200 for up to four traffic offenses, $100 for every traffic offense thereafter, $100 for every Failure to Appear charge, and $300 for every criminal offense, FPD's own policy includes a bond schedule that departs from these figures. In practice, bond amounts vary widely. *See* FPD General Order 421.02. Our review of a random sample of warrants indicates that bond is set in a manner that often departs from both the schedule referenced by court staff and the schedule found in FPD policy. In a number of these cases, the bond amount far exceeded the amount of the underlying fine.

The court's bond practices, including the fact that the court often imposes bonds that exceed the amount owed to the court, do not appear to be grounded in any public safety need. In a July 2014 email to Chief Jackson and other police officials, the Court Clerk reported that "[s]tarting today we are going to reduce anyone's bond that calls and is in warrant[] to half the amount," explaining that "[t]his may bring in some extra monies this way." The email identifies no public safety obstacle or other reason not to implement the bond reduction. Notably, the email also states that "[w]e will only do this between the hours of 8:30 to 4" and that no halfbond will be accepted after those hours unless the Court Clerk approves it.[36] Thus, as a result of this policy, an individual able to appear at the court window during business hours would pay half as much to clear a warrant as an individual who is actually arrested on a warrant after hours. That Ferguson's bond practices do not appear grounded in public safety is underscored by the fact that the court will typically cancel outstanding warrants without requiring the posting of *any* bond for people who have an attorney enter an appearance on their behalf. Records show that this practice is also applied haphazardly, and there do not appear to be any rules that govern the apparent discretion court staff have to waive or require bond following an attorney's appearance.

It is not uncommon for an individual charged with only a minor violation to be arrested on a warrant, be unable to afford bond, and have no recourse but to await release. Longstanding court rules provide for a person arrested pursuant to an arrest warrant to be held up to 72 hours before being released without bond, and the court's recent orders do not appear to change this. Records show that individuals are routinely held for 72 hours. FPD's records management system only began capturing meaningful jail data in April 2014; but from April to September 2014 alone, 77 people were detained in the jail for longer than two days, and many of those detentions neared, reached, or exceeded the 72-hour mark. Of those 77 people, 73, or 95%, were black. Many people, including the woman described earlier who was charged with two parking code violations, have reported being held up until the 72-hour limit—despite having no ability to pay.

Indeed, many others report being held for far longer, and documentary evidence is consistent with these reports. In April 2010, for example, the Chief of Police wrote an email to the Captain of the Patrol Division stating that the "intent is that when the watch commander / street supervisor gets the census from the jail he asks who will come up on 72 hrs.," and, if there is any such person, "he can have them given the next available court date and released, or authorize they remain in jail, since he will be the designate."

The email continues: "If someone has already been there more than 72 hours, it may be assumed their continued hold was previously authorized." Further, as noted above, while comprehensive jail records do not exist for detentions prior to April 2014, records do show several recent instances in which FPD detained a person for longer than the purported 72-hour limit.

Despite the fact that those arrested by FPD for outstanding municipal warrants can be held for several days if unable to post bond, the Ferguson municipal court does not give credit for time served. As a result, there have been many cases in which a person has been arrested on a warrant, detained for 72 hours or more, and released owing the same amount as before the arrest was made. Court records do not even track the total amount of time a person has spent in jail as part of a case. When asked why this is not tracked, a member of court staff told us: "It's only three days anyway."

These prolonged detentions for those who cannot afford bond are alarming, and raise considerable due process and equal protection concerns. The prolonged detentions are especially concerning given that there is no public safety need for those who receive municipal warrants to be jailed at all. The Ferguson Municipal Judge has acknowledged that for most code violations, it is "probably a good idea to do away with jail time."

Further, there are many circumstances in which court practices preclude a person from making payment against the underlying fine owed—and thus resolving the case, or at least moving the case toward resolution— and instead force the person to pay a bond. If, for example, an individual is jailed on a "must appear" charge and has not yet appeared in court to have the fine assessed, the individual will not be allowed to make payment on the underlying charge. Rather, the person must post bond, receive a new court date, appear in court, and start the process anew. Even when the underlying fine has been assessed, a person in jail may still be forced to make a bond payment instead of a fine payment to secure release if court staff are unavailable to determine the amount the person owes. And when a person attempts to resolve a warrant before they end up arrested, a bond payment will typically be required unless the person can afford to pay the underlying fine in full, as, by purported policy, the court does not accept partial payment of fines outside of a court-sanctioned payment plan.

Bond forfeiture procedures also raise significant due process concerns. Under current practice, the first missed appearance or missed payment following a bond payment results in a warning letter being sent; after the second missed appearance or payment, the court initiates a forfeiture action (and issues another arrest warrant). As with "warrant warning letters" described above, our investigation has been unable to verify that the court *consistently* sends bond forfeiture warning letters. And, as with warrant warning letters, bond forfeiture warning letters are sometimes returned to the court, but court staff members do not appear to make any further attempt to contact the intended recipient.

Upon a bond being forfeited, the court directs the bond money into the City's account and does not apply the amount to the individual's underlying fine. For example, if a person owes a $200 fine payment, is arrested on a warrant, and posts a bond of $200, the forfeiture of the bond will result in the fine remaining $200 and an arrest warrant being issued. If, instead, Ferguson were to allow this $200 to go toward the underlying fine, this would resolve the matter entirely, obviating the need for any warrant or subsequent court appearance. Not applying a forfeited bond to the underlying fine is especially troubling considering that this policy does not appear to be clearly communicated to those paying bonds. Particularly in cases where the bond is set at an amount near the underlying fine owed—which we have found to be common—it is entirely plausible that a person paying bond would mistakenly believe that payment resolves the case.

When asked why the forfeited bond is not applied to the underlying fine, court staff asserted that applicable law prohibits them from doing so without the bond payer's consent.[37] That explanation is grounded in an incorrect view of the law. In *Perry v. Aversman*, 168 S.W.3d 541 (Mo. Ct. App. 2005), the Missouri Court of Appeals explicitly upheld a rule requiring that forfeited bonds be applied to pending fines of the person who paid bond and found that such practices are acceptable so long as the court provides sufficient notice. *Id.* at 543-46. In light of the fact that applicable law permits forfeited bonds to be applied to pending fines, Ferguson's long-standing practice of directing forfeited bond money to the City's general fund is troubling. In fiscal year 2013 alone, the City collected forfeited bond amounts of $177,168, which could instead have been applied to the fines of those making the payments.

Ferguson's rules and procedures for *refunding* bond payments upon satisfaction of the underlying fine raise similar concerns. Ferguson requires that when a person pays the underlying fine to avoid bond forfeiture, he or she must pay in person and provide photo identification. Yet, where the underlying fine is less than the bond amount—a common occurrence—the City does not immediately refund the difference to the individual. Rather, pursuant to a directive issued by the current City Finance Director approximately four years ago, bond refunds *cannot* be made in person, and instead must be sent via mail. According to Ferguson's Court Clerk, it is not entirely uncommon for these refund checks to be returned as undeliverable and become "unclaimed property."

C. Ferguson Law Enforcement Practices Disproportionately Harm Ferguson's African-American Residents and Are Driven in Part by Racial Bias

Ferguson's police and municipal court practices disproportionately harm African Americans. Further, our investigation found substantial evidence that this harm stems in part from intentional discrimination in violation of the Constitution.

African Americans experience disparate impact in nearly every aspect of Ferguson's law enforcement system. Despite making up 67% of the population, African Americans accounted for 85% of FPD's traffic stops, 90% of FPD's citations, and 93% of FPD's arrests from 2012 to 2014. Other statistical disparities, set forth in detail below, show that in Ferguson:

- African Americans are 2.07 times more likely to be searched during a vehicular stop but are 26% less likely to have contraband found on them during a search. They are 2.00 times more likely to receive a citation and 2.37 times more likely to be arrested following a vehicular stop.

- African Americans have force used against them at disproportionately high rates, accounting for 88% of all cases from 2010 to August 2014 in which an FPD officer reported using force. In all 14 uses of force involving a canine bite for which we have information about the race of the person bitten, the person was African American.

- African Americans are more likely to receive multiple citations during a single incident, receiving four or more citations on 73 occasions between October 2012 and July 2014, whereas non-African Americans received four or more citations only twice during that period.

- African Americans account for 95% of Manner of Walking charges; 94% of all Fail to Comply charges; 92% of all Resisting Arrest charges; 92% of all Peace Disturbance charges; and 89% of all Failure to Obey charges.[38]

- African Americans are 68% less likely than others to have their cases dismissed by the Municipal Judge, and in 2013 African Americans accounted for 92% of cases in which an arrest warrant was issued.

- African Americans account for 96% of known arrests made exclusively because of an outstanding municipal warrant.

These disparities are not the necessary or unavoidable results of legitimate public safety efforts. In fact, the practices that lead to these disparities in many ways undermine law enforcement effectiveness. *See, e.g.,* Jack Glaser, *Suspect Race: Causes and Consequence of Racial Profiling* 96–126 (2015) (because profiling can increase crime while harming communities, it has a "high risk" of contravening the core police objectives of controlling crime and promoting public safety). The disparate impact of these practices thus violates federal law, including Title VI and the Safe Streets Act.

The racially disparate impact of Ferguson's practices is driven, at least in part, by intentional discrimination in violation of the Equal Protection Clause of the Fourteenth Amendment. Racial bias and stereotyping is evident from the facts, taken together. This evidence includes: the consistency and magnitude of the racial disparities throughout Ferguson's police and court enforcement actions; the selection and execution of police and court practices that disproportionately harm African Americans and do little to promote public safety; the persistent exercise of discretion to the detriment of African Americans; the apparent consideration of race in assessing threat; and the historical opposition to having African Americans live in Ferguson, which lingers among some today. We have also found explicit racial bias in the communications of police and court supervisors and that some officials apply racial stereotypes, rather than facts, to explain the harm African Americans experience due to Ferguson's approach to law enforcement. "Determining whether invidious discriminatory purpose was a motivating factor demands a sensitive inquiry into such circumstantial and direct evidence of intent as may be available." *Vill. of Arlington Heights v. Metro. Hous. Dev. Corp.*, 429 U.S. 252, 266 (1977). Based on this evidence as a whole, we have found that Ferguson's law enforcement activities stem in part from a discriminatory purpose and thus deny African Americans equal protection of the laws in violation of the Constitution.

1. FERGUSON'S LAW ENFORCEMENT ACTIONS IMPOSE A DISPARATE IMPACT ON AFRICAN AMERICANS THAT VIOLATES FEDERAL LAW

African Americans are disproportionately represented at nearly every stage of Ferguson law enforcement, from initial police contact to final disposition of a case in municipal court. While FPD's data collection and retention practices are deficient in many respects, the data that is collected by FPD is sufficient to allow for meaningful and reliable analysis of racial disparities. This data—collected directly by police and court officials—reveals racial disparities that are substantial and consistent across a wide range of police and court enforcement actions.

African Americans experience the harms of the disparities identified below as part of a comprehensive municipal justice system that, at each juncture, enforces the law more harshly against black people than others. The disparate impact of Ferguson's enforcement actions is compounding: at each point in the enforcement process there is a higher likelihood that an African American will be subjected to harsher treatment; accordingly, as the adverse consequences imposed by Ferguson grow more and more severe, those consequences are imposed more and more disproportionately against African Americans. Thus, while 85% of FPD's vehicle stops are of African Americans, 90% of FPD's citations are issued to African Americans, and 92% of all warrants are issued in cases against African Americans. Strikingly, available data shows that of those subjected to one of the most severe actions this system routinely imposes—actual arrest for an outstanding municipal warrant—96% are African American.

a. Disparate Impact of FPD Practices

i. Disparate Impact of FPD Enforcement Actions Arising from
Vehicular Stops

Pursuant to Missouri state law on racial profiling, Mo. Rev. Stat. § 590.650, FPD officers are required to collect race and other data during every traffic stop. While some law enforcement agencies collect more comprehensive data to identify and stem racial profiling, this information is sufficient to show that FPD practices exert a racially disparate impact along several dimensions.

FPD reported 11,610 vehicle stops between October 2012 and October 2014. African Americans accounted for 85%, or 9,875, of those stops, despite making up only 67% of the population. White individuals made up 15%, or 1,735, of stops during that period, despite representing 29% of the population. These differences indicate that FPD traffic *stop* practices may disparately impact black drivers.[39] Even setting aside the question of whether there are racial disparities in FPD's traffic stop practices, however, the data collected during those stops reliably shows statistically significant racial disparities in the *outcomes* people receive *after* being stopped. Unlike with vehicle stops, assessing the disparate impact of post-stop outcomes—such as the rate at which stops result in citations, searches, or arrests—is not dependent on population data or on assumptions about differential offending rates by race; instead, the enforcement actions imposed against stopped black drivers are compared directly to the enforcement actions imposed against stopped white drivers.

In Ferguson, traffic stops of black drivers are more likely to lead to searches, citations, and arrests than are stops of white drivers. Black people are significantly more likely to be searched during a traffic stop than white people. From October 2012 to October 2014, 11% of stopped black drivers were searched, whereas only 5% of stopped white drivers were searched.

Despite being searched at higher rates, African Americans are 26% *less* likely to have contraband found on them than whites: 24% of searches of African Americans resulted in a contraband finding, whereas 30% of searches of whites resulted in a contraband finding. This disparity exists even after controlling for the type of search conducted, whether a search incident to arrest, a consent search, or a search predicated on reasonable suspicion. The lower rate at which officers find contraband when searching African Americans indicates either that officers' suspicion of criminal wrongdoing is less likely to be accurate when interacting with African Americans or that officers are more likely to search African Americans without any suspicion of criminal wrongdoing. Either explanation suggests bias, whether explicit or implicit.[40] This lower hit rate for African Americans also underscores that this disparate enforcement practice is ineffective.

Other, more subtle indicators likewise show meaningful disparities in FPD's search practices: of the 31 *Terry* stop searches FPD conducted during this period between October 2012 to October 2014, 30 were of black individuals; of the 103 times FPD asked both the driver and passenger to exit a vehicle during a search, the searched individuals were black in 95 cases; and, while only one search of a white person lasted more than half an hour (1% of all searches of white drivers), 59 searches of African Americans lasted that long (5% of all searches of black drivers).

Of all stopped black drivers, 91%, or 8,987, received citations, while 87%, or 1,501, of all stopped white drivers received a citation.[41] 891 stopped black drivers—10% of all stopped black drivers—were arrested as a result of the stop, whereas only 63 stopped white drivers—4% of all stopped white drivers—were arrested. This disparity is explainable in large part by the high number of black individuals arrested for outstanding municipal warrants issued for missed court payments and appearances. As we discuss below, African Americans are more likely to have warrants issued against them than whites and are more likely to be arrested for an outstanding warrant than their white counterparts. Notably, on 14 occasions FPD listed the only reason for an arrest following a traffic stop as "resisting arrest." In all 14 of those cases, the person arrested was black.

These disparities in the outcomes that result from traffic stops remain even after regression analysis is used to control for non-race-based variables, including driver age; gender; the assignment of the officer making the stop; disparities in officer behavior; and the stated reason the stop was initiated. Upon accounting for differences in those variables, African Americans remained 2.07 times more likely to be searched; 2.00 times more likely to receive a citation; and 2.37 times more likely to be arrested than other stopped individuals. Each of these disparities is statistically significant and would occur by chance less than one time in 1,000.[42] The odds of these disparities occurring by chance together are significantly lower still.

ii. Disparate Impact of FPD's Multiple Citation Practices

The substantial racial disparities that exist within the data collected from traffic stops are consistent with the disparities found throughout FPD's practices. As discussed above, our investigation found that FPD officers frequently make discretionary choices to issue multiple citations during a single incident. Setting aside the fact that, in some cases, citations are redundant and impose duplicative penalties for the same offense, the issuance of multiples citations also disproportionately impacts African Americans.

In 2013, for instance, more than 50% of all African Americans cited received multiple citations during a single encounter with FPD, whereas only 26% of non-African Americans did. Specifically, 26% of African Americans receiving a citation received two citations at once, whereas only 17% of white individuals received two citations at once. Those disparities are even greater for incidents that resulted in more than two citations: 15% of African Americans cited received three citations at the same time, whereas 6% of cited whites received three citations; and while 10% of cited African Americans received four or more citations at once, only 3% of cited whites received that many during a single incident. Each of these disparities is statistically significant, and would occur by chance less than one time in 1,000. Indeed, related data from an overlapping time period shows that, between October 2012 to July 2014, 38 black individuals received four citations during a single incident, compared with only two white individuals; and while 35 black individuals received five or more citations at once, not a single white person did.[43]

iii. Disparate Impact of Other FPD Charging Practices

From October 2012 to July 2014, African Americans accounted for 85%, or 30,525, of the 35,871 *total* charges brought by FPD—including traffic citations, summonses, and arrests. Non-African Americans accounted for 15%, or 5,346, of all charges brought during that period.[44] These rates vary somewhat across different offenses. For example, African Americans represent a relatively low proportion of those charged with Driving While Intoxicated and Speeding on State Roads or Highways. With respect to speeding offenses for all roads, African Americans account for 72% of citations based on radar or laser, but 80% of citations based on other or unspecified methods. Thus, as evaluated by radar, African Americans violate the law at lower rates than as evaluated by FPD officers. Indeed, controlling for other factors, the disparity in speeding tickets between African Americans and non-African Americans is 48% larger when citations are issued not on the basis of radar or laser, but by some other method, such as the officer's own visual assessment. This difference is statistically significant.

Data on charges issued by FPD from 2011–2013 shows that, for numerous municipal offenses for which FPD officers have a high degree of discretion in charging, African Americans are disproportionately represented relative to their representation in Ferguson's population. While African Americans make up 67% of Ferguson's population, they make up 95% of Manner of Walking in Roadway charges; 94% of Failure to Comply charges; 92% of Resisting Arrest charges; 92% of Peace Disturbance charges; and 89% of Failure to Obey charges. Because these non-traffic offenses are more likely to be brought against persons who actually live in Ferguson than are vehicle stops, census data here does provide a useful benchmark for whether a pattern of racially disparate policing appears to exist. These disparities mean that African Americans in Ferguson bear the overwhelming burden of FPD's pattern of unlawful stops, searches, and arrests with respect to these highly discretionary ordinances.

iv. Disparate Impact of FPD Arrests for Outstanding Warrants

FPD records show that once a warrant issues, racial disparities in FPD's warrant execution practices make it exceedingly more likely for a black individual with an outstanding warrant to be arrested than a white individual with an outstanding warrant. Arrest data captured by FPD often fails to identify when a person is arrested *solely* on account of an outstanding warrant. Nonetheless, the data FPD collects during traffic stops pursuant to Missouri state requirements does capture information regarding when arrests are made for no other reason than that an arrest warrant was pending. Based upon that data, from October 2012 to October 2014, FPD arrested 460 individuals exclusively because the person had an outstanding arrest warrant. Of those 460 people arrested, 443, or 96%, were black. That African Americans are disproportionately impacted by FPD's warrant execution practices is also reflected in the fact that, during the roughly six-month period from April to September 2014, African Americans accounted for 96% of those booked into the Ferguson City Jail at least *in part* because they were arrested for an outstanding municipal warrant.

v. Concerns Regarding Pedestrian Stops

Although available data enables an assessment of the disparate impact of many FPD practices, many other practices cannot be assessed statistically because of FPD's inadequate data collection. FPD does not reliably collect or track data regarding pedestrian stops, or FPD officers' conduct during those stops. Given this lack of data, we are unable to determine whether African Americans are disproportionately the subjects of pedestrian stops, or the rate of searches, arrests, or other post-pedestrian stop outcomes. We note, however, that during our investigation we have spoken with not only black community members who have been stopped by FPD officers, but also non-black community members and employees of local businesses who have observed FPD conduct pedestrian stops of others, all of whom universally report that pedestrian stops in Ferguson almost always involve African-American youth. Even though FPD does not specifically track pedestrian stops, other FPD records are consistent with those accounts. Arrest and other incident reports sometimes describe encounters that begin with pedestrian stops, almost all of which involve African Americans.

b. Disparate Impact of Court Practices

Our investigation has also found that the rules and practices of the Ferguson municipal court also exert a disparate impact on African Americans. As discussed above, once a charge is filed in Ferguson municipal court, a number of procedural barriers imposed by the court combine to make it unnecessarily difficult to resolve the charge. Data created and maintained by the court show that black defendants are significantly more likely to be adversely impacted by those barriers. An assessment of every charge filed in Ferguson municipal court in 2011 shows that, over time, black defendants are more likely to have their cases persist for longer durations, more likely to face a higher number of mandatory court appearances and other requirements, and more likely to have a warrant issued against them for failing to meet those requirements.[45]

In light of the opaque court procedures previously discussed, the likelihood of running afoul of a court requirement increases when a case lasts for a longer period of time and results in more court encounters. Court cases involving black individuals typically last longer than those involving white individuals. Of the 2,369 charges filed against white defendants in 2011, over 63% were closed after six months. By contrast, only 34% of the 10,984 charges against black defendants were closed within that time period. 10% of black defendants, however, resolved their case between six months and a year from when it was filed, while 9% of white defendants required that much time to secure resolution. And, while 17% of black defendants resolved their charge over a year after it was brought against them, only 9% of white defendants required that much time. Each of these cases was ultimately resolved, in most instances by satisfying debts owed to the court; but this data shows substantial disparities between blacks and whites regarding how long it took to do so.

On average, African Americans are also more likely to have a high number of "events" occur before a case is resolved. The court's records track all activities that occur in a case—from payments and court appearances to continuances and Failure to Appear charges. 11% of cases involving African Americans had three "events," whereas 10% of cases involving white defendants had three events. 14% of cases involving black defendants had four to five events, compared with 9% of cases involving white defendants. Those disparities increase as the recorded number of events per case increases. Data show that there are ten or more events in 17% of cases involving black defendants but only 5% of cases involving white defendants. Given that an "event" can represent a variety of different kinds of occurrences, these particular disparities are perhaps less probative; nonetheless, they strongly suggest that black defendants have, on average, more encounters with the court during a single case than their white peers.

Given the figures above, it is perhaps unsurprising that the municipal court's practice of issuing warrants to compel fine payments following a missed court appearance or missed payment has a disparate impact on black defendants. 92% of all warrants issued in 2013 were issued in cases involving an African-American defendant. This figure is disproportionate to the representation of African Americans in the court's docket. Although the

proportion of court cases involving black defendants has increased in recent years—81% of all cases filed in 2009, compared with 85% of all cases
filed in 2013—that proportion remains substantially below the proportion
of warrants issued to African Americans.

These disparities are consistent with the evidence discussed above that
African Americans are often unable to resolve municipal charges despite
taking appropriate steps to do so, and the evidence discussed below suggesting that court officials exercise discretion in a manner that disadvan-
tages the African Americans that appear before the court.

Notably, the evidence suggests that African Americans are not only
disparately impacted by court procedures, but also by the court's discretionary rulings in individual cases. Although court data did not enable a
comprehensive assessment of disparities in fines that the court imposes,
we did review fine data regarding ten different offenses and offense categories, including the five highly discretionary offenses disproportionately
brought against African Americans noted above.[46] That analysis suggests
that there may be racial disparities in the court's fine assessment practices.
In analyzing the initial fines assessed for those ten offenses for each year
from 2011–2013—30 data points in total—the average fine assessment
was higher for African Americans than others in 26 of the 30 data points.
For example, among the 53 Failure to Obey charges brought in 2013 that
did not lead to added Failure to Appear fines—44 of which involved an
African-American defendant—African Americans were assessed an average fine of $206, whereas the average fine for others was $147. The magnitude of racial disparities in fine amounts varied across the 30 yearly offense
averages analyzed, but those disparities consistently disfavored African
Americans.

Further, an evaluation of dismissal rates throughout the life of a case
shows that, on average, an African-American defendant is 68% less likely
than other defendants to have a case dismissed. In addition to cases that are
"Dismissed," court records also show cases that are "Voided" altogether.
There are only roughly 400 cases listed as Voided from 2011–2013, but the
data that is available for that relatively small number of Voided cases shows

that African Americans are three times less likely to receive the Voided outcome than others.

c. Ferguson's Racially Disparate Practices Violate Federal Law

This data shows that police and court practices impose a disparate impact on black individuals that itself violates the law. Title VI and the Safe Streets Act prohibit law enforcement agencies that receive federal financial assistance, such as FPD, from engaging in law enforcement activities that have an unnecessary disparate impact based on race, color, or national origin. 42 U.S.C. § 2000d. Title VI's implementing regulations prohibit law enforcement agencies from using "criteria or methods of administration" that have an unnecessary disparate impact based on race, color, or national origin. 28 C.F.R. § 42.104(b)(2); *see also Alexander v. Sandoval*, 532 U.S. 275, 281-82 (2001). Similarly, the Safe Streets Act applies not only to intentional discrimination, but also to any law enforcement practices that unnecessarily disparately impact an identified group based on the enumerated factors. 28 C.F.R. § 42.203. *Cf. Charleston Housing Authority v. USDA*, 419 F.3d 729, 741-42 (8th Cir. 2005) (finding in the related Fair Housing Act context that where official action imposes a racially disparate impact, the action can only be justified through a showing that it is necessary to nondiscriminatory objectives).

Thus, under these statutes, the discriminatory impact of Ferguson's law enforcement practices—which is both unnecessary and avoidable—is unlawful regardless of whether it is intentional or not. As set forth below, these practices also violate the prohibitions against intentional discrimination contained within Title VI, the Safe Streets Act, and the Fourteenth Amendment.

2. FERGUSON'S LAW ENFORCEMENT PRACTICES ARE MOTIVATED IN PART BY DISCRIMINATORY INTENT IN VIOLATION OF THE FOURTEENTH AMENDMENT AND OTHER FEDERAL LAWS

The race-based disparities created by Ferguson's law enforcement practices cannot be explained by chance or by any difference in the rates at which people of different races adhere to the law. These disparities occur, at least in part, because Ferguson law enforcement practices are directly shaped and perpetuated by racial bias. Those practices thus operate in violation of the Fourteenth Amendment's Equal Protection Clause, which prohibits discriminatory policing on the basis of race. *Whren*, 517 U.S. at 813; *Johnson v. Crooks*, 326 F.3d 995, 999 (8th Cir. 2003).[47]

An Equal Protection Clause violation can occur where, as here, the official administration of facially neutral laws or policies results in a discriminatory effect that is motivated, at least in part, by a discriminatory purpose. *See Washington v. Davis*, 426 U.S. 229, 239-40 (1976). In assessing whether a given practice stems from a discriminatory purpose, courts conduct a "sensitive inquiry into such circumstantial and direct evidence of intent as may be available," including historical background, contemporaneous statements by decision makers, and substantive departures from normal procedure. *Vill. of Arlington Heights*, 429 U.S. at 266; *United States v. Bell*, 86 F.3d 820, 823 (8th Cir. 1996). To violate the Equal Protection Clause, official action need not rest solely on racially discriminatory purposes; rather, official action violates the Equal Protection Clause if it is motivated, at least in part, by discriminatory purpose. *Personnel Adm'r of Mass. v. Feeney*, 442 U.S. 256, 279 (1979).

We have uncovered significant evidence showing that racial bias has impermissibly played a role in shaping the actions of police and court officials in Ferguson. That evidence, detailed below, includes: 1) the consistency and magnitude of the racial disparities found throughout police and court enforcement actions; 2) direct communications by police supervisors and court officials that exhibit racial bias, particularly against African Americans; 3) a number of other communications by police and court officials that reflect harmful racial stereotypes; 4) the background and historic context surrounding FPD's racially disparate enforcement practices; 5) the fact that City, police, and court officials failed to take any meaningful steps to evaluate or address the race-based impact of its law enforcement practices despite longstanding and widely reported racial disparities, and instead consistently reapplied police and court practices known to disparately impact African Americans.

a. Consistency and Magnitude of Identified Racial Disparities

In assessing whether an official action was motivated in part by discriminatory intent, the actual impact of the action and whether it "bears more heavily on one race or another" may "provide an important starting point." *Vill. of Arlington Heights*, 429 U.S. at 266 (internal citations and quotation marks omitted). Indeed, in rare cases, statistical evidence of discriminatory impact may be sufficiently probative to itself establish discriminatory intent. *Hazelwood School Dist. v. United States*, 433 U.S. 299, 307-08 (1977) (noting in the Title VII context that where "gross statistical disparities can be shown, they alone may in a proper case constitute prima facie proof of a pattern or practice of discrimination").

The race-based disparities we have found are not isolated or aberrational; rather, they exist in nearly every aspect of Ferguson police and court operations. As discussed above, statistical analysis shows that African Americans are more likely to be searched but less likely to have contraband found on them; more likely to receive a citation following a stop and more likely to receive multiple citations at once; more likely to be arrested; more likely to have force used against them; more likely to have their case last longer and require more encounters with the municipal court; more likely to have an arrest warrant issued against them by the municipal court; and more likely to be arrested solely on the basis of an outstanding warrant. As noted above, many of these disparities would occur by chance less than one time in 1000.

These disparities provide significant evidence of discriminatory intent, as the "impact of an official action is often probative of why the action was taken in the first place since people usually intend the natural consequences of their actions." *Reno v. Bossier Parish Sch. Bd.*, 520 U.S. 471, 487 (1997); *see also Davis*, 426 U.S. at 242 ("An invidious discriminatory purpose may often be inferred from the totality of the relevant facts, including the fact, if it is true, that the [practice] bears more heavily on one race than another."). These disparities are unexplainable on grounds other than race and evidence that racial bias, whether implicit or explicit, has shaped law enforcement conduct.[48]

b. Direct Evidence of Racial Bias

Our investigation uncovered direct evidence of racial bias in the communications of influential Ferguson decision makers. In email messages and during interviews, several court and law enforcement personnel expressed discriminatory views and intolerance with regard to race, religion, and national origin. The content of these communications is unequivocally derogatory, dehumanizing, and demonstrative of impermissible bias.

We have discovered evidence of racial bias in emails sent by Ferguson officials, all of whom are current employees, almost without exception through their official City of Ferguson email accounts, and apparently sent during work hours. These email exchanges involved several police and court supervisors, including FPD supervisors and commanders. The following emails are illustrative:

- A November 2008 email stated that President Barack Obama would not be President for very long because "what black man holds a steady job for four years."

- A March 2010 email mocked African Americans through speech and familial stereotypes, using a story involving child support. One line from the email read: "I be so glad that dis be my last child support payment! Month after month, year after year, all dose payments!"

- An April 2011 email depicted President Barack Obama as a chimpanzee.

- A May 2011 email stated: "An African-American woman in New Orleans was admitted into the hospital for a pregnancy termination. Two weeks later she received a check for $5,000. She phoned the hospital to ask who it was from. The hospital said, 'Crimestoppers.'"

- A June 2011 email described a man seeking to obtain "welfare" for his dogs because they are "mixed in color, unemployed, lazy, can't speak English and have no frigging clue who their Daddies are."

- An October 2011 email included a photo of a bare-chested group of dancing women, apparently in Africa, with the caption, "Michelle Obama's High School Reunion."
- A December 2011 email included jokes that are based on offensive stereotypes about Muslims.

Our review of documents revealed many additional email communications that exhibited racial or ethnic bias, as well as other forms of bias. Our investigation has not revealed any indication that any officer or court clerk engaged in these communications was ever disciplined. Nor did we see a single instance in which a police or court recipient of such an email asked that the sender refrain from sending such emails, or any indication that these emails were reported as inappropriate. Instead, the emails were usually forwarded along to others.[49]

Critically, each of these email exchanges involved supervisors of FPD's patrol and court operations.[50] FPD patrol supervisors are responsible for holding officers accountable to governing laws, including the Constitution, and helping to ensure that officers treat all people equally under the law, regardless of race or any other protected characteristic. The racial animus and stereotypes expressed by these supervisors suggest that they are unlikely to hold an officer accountable for discriminatory conduct or to take any steps to discourage the development or perpetuation of racial stereotypes among officers.

Similarly, court supervisors have significant influence and discretion in managing the court's operations and in processing individual cases. As discussed in Parts I and III.B of this report, our investigation has found that a number of court rules and procedures are interpreted and applied entirely at the discretion of the court clerks. These include: whether to require a court appearance for certain offenses; whether to grant continuances or other procedural requests; whether to accept partial payment of an owed fine; whether to cancel a warrant without a bond payment; and whether to provide individuals with documentation enabling them to have a suspended driver's license reinstated before the full fine owed has been paid off. Court clerks are also largely responsible for setting bond amounts. The evidence we found thus shows not only racial bias, but racial bias by those with considerable influence over the outcome of any given court case.

This documentary evidence of explicit racial bias is consistent with re-ports from community members indicating that some FPD officers use ra-cial epithets in dealing with members of the public. We spoke with one African-American man who, in August 2014, had an argument in his apart-ment to which FPD officers responded, and was immediately pulled out of the apartment by force. After telling the officer, "you don't have a reason to lock me up," he claims the officer responded: "N*****, I can find something to lock you up on." When the man responded, "good luck with that," the officer slammed his face into the wall, and after the man fell to the floor, the officer said, "don't pass out motherf****r because I'm not carrying you to my car." Another young man described walking with friends in July 2014 past a group of FPD officers who shouted racial epithets at them as they passed.

Courts have widely acknowledged that direct statements exhibiting ra-cial bias are exceedingly rare, and that such statements are not necessary for establishing the existence of discriminatory purpose. *See, e.g., Hayden v. Paterson*, 594 F.3d 150, 163 (2d Cir. 2010) (noting that "discriminatory intent is rarely susceptible to direct proof"); *see also Thomas v. Eastman Kodak Co.*, 183 F.3d 38, 64 (1st Cir. 1999) (noting in Title VII case that "[t]here is no requirement that a plaintiff . . . must present direct, 'smoking gun' evidence of racially biased decision making in order to prevail"); *Rob-inson v. Runyon*, 149 F.3d 507, 513 (6th Cir. 1998) (noting in Title VII case that "[r]arely will there be direct evidence from the lips of the defendant proclaiming his or her racial animus"). Where such evidence does exist, however, it is highly probative of discriminatory intent. That is particularly true where, as here, the communications exhibiting bias are made by those with considerable decision-making authority. *See Doe v. Mamaroneck*, 462 F. Supp. 2d 520, 550 (S.D.N.Y. 2006); *Eberhart v. Gettys*, 215 F. Supp. 2d 666, 678 (M.D.N.C. 2002).

c. Evidence of Racial Stereotyping

Several Ferguson officials told us during our investigation that it is a lack of "personal responsibility" among African-American members of the Ferguson community that causes African Americans to experience disproportionate harm under Ferguson's approach to law enforcement. Our investigation suggests that this explanation is at odd with the facts. While there are people of all races who may lack personal responsibility, the harm of Ferguson's approach to law enforcement is largely due to the myriad systemic deficiencies discussed above. Our investigation revealed African Americans making extraordinary efforts to pay off expensive tickets for minor, often unfairly charged, violations, despite systemic obstacles to resolving those tickets. While our investigation did not indicate that African Americans are disproportionately irresponsible, it did reveal that, as the above emails reflect, some Ferguson decision makers hold negative stereotypes about African Americans, and lack of personal responsibility is one of them. Application of this stereotype furthers the disproportionate impact of Ferguson's police and court practices. It causes court and police decision makers to discredit African Americans' explanations for not being able to pay tickets and allows officials to disown the harms of Ferguson's law enforcement practices.

The common practice among Ferguson officials of writing off tickets further evidences a double standard grounded in racial stereotyping. Even as Ferguson City officials maintain the harmful stereotype that black individuals lack personal responsibility—and continue to cite this lack of personal responsibility as the cause of the disparate impact of Ferguson's practices—white City officials condone a striking lack of personal responsibility among themselves and their friends. Court records and emails show City officials, including the Municipal Judge, the Court Clerk, and FPD supervisors assisting friends, colleagues, acquaintances, and themselves in eliminating citations, fines, and fees. For example:

- In August 2014, the Court Clerk emailed Municipal Judge Brockmeyer a copy of a Failure to Appear notice for a speeding violation issued by the City of Breckenridge, and asked: "[FPD patrol supervisor] came to me this morning, could you please take [care] of this for him in Breckenridge?" The Judge replied: "Sure." Judge Brockmeyer also serves as Municipal Judge in Breckenridge.

- In October 2013, Judge Brockmeyer sent Ferguson's Prosecuting Attorney an email with the subject line "City of Hazelwood vs. Ronald Brockmeyer." The Judge wrote: "Pursuant to our conversation, attached please find the red light camera ticket received by the undersigned. I would appreciate it if you would please see to it that this ticket is dismissed." The Prosecuting Attorney, who also serves as prosecuting attorney in Hazelwood, responded: "I worked on red light matters today and dismissed the ticket that you sent over. Since I entered that into the system today, you may or may not get a second notice—you can just ignore that."

- In August 2013, an FPD patrol supervisor wrote an email entitled "Oops" to the Prosecuting Attorney regarding a ticket his relative received in another municipality for traveling 59 miles per hour in a 40 miles-per-hour zone, noting "[h]aving it dismissed would be a blessing." The Prosecuting Attorney responded that the prosecutor of that other municipality promised to nolle pros the ticket. The supervisor responded with appreciation, noting that the dismissal "[c]ouldn't have come at a better time."

- Also in August 2013, Ferguson's Mayor emailed the Prosecuting Attorney about a parking ticket received by an employee of a non-profit day camp for which the Mayor sometimes volunteers. The Mayor wrote that the person "shouldn't have left his car unattended there, but it was an honest mistake" and stated, "I would hate for him to have to pay for this, can you help?" The Prosecuting Attorney forwarded the email to the Court Clerk, instructing her to "NP [nolle prosequi, or not prosecute] this parking ticket."

- In November 2011, a court clerk received a request from a friend to "fix a parking ticket" received by the friend's coworker's wife. After the ticket was faxed to the clerk, she replied: "It's gone baby!"
- In March 2014, a friend of the Court Clerk's relative emailed the Court Clerk with a scanned copy of a ticket asking if there was anything she could do to help. She responded: "Your ticket of $200 has magically disappeared!" Later, in June 2014, the same person emailed the Court Clerk regarding two tickets and asked: "Can you work your magic again? It would be deeply appreciated." The Clerk later informed him one ticket had been dismissed and she was waiting to hear back about the second ticket.

These are just a few illustrative examples. It is clear that writing off tickets between the Ferguson court staff and the clerks of other municipal courts in the region is routine. Email exchanges show that Ferguson officials secured or received ticket write-offs from staff in a number of neighboring municipalities. There is evidence that the Court Clerk and a City of Hazelwood clerk "fixed" at least 12 tickets at each other's request, and that the Court Clerk successfully sought help with a ticket from a clerk in St. Ann. And in April 2011, a court administrator in the City of Pine Lawn emailed the Ferguson Court Clerk to have a warrant recalled for a person applying for a job with the Pine Lawn Police Department. The court administrator explained that "[a]fter he gets the job, he will have money to pay off his fines with Ferguson." The Court Clerk recalled the warrant and issued a new court date for more than two months after the request was made.

City officials' application of the stereotype that African Americans lack "personal responsibility" to explain why Ferguson's practices harm African Americans, even as these same City officials exhibit a lack of personal— and professional—responsibility in handling their own and their friends' code violations, is further evidence of discriminatory bias on the part of decision makers central to the direction of law enforcement in Ferguson.

d. Historical Background

Until the 1960s, Ferguson was a "sundown town" where African Americans were banned from the City after dark. The City would block off the main road from Kinloch, which was a poor, all-black suburb, "with a chain and construction materials but kept a second road open during the day so housekeepers and nannies could get from Kinloch to jobs in Ferguson."[51] During our investigative interviews, several older African-American residents recalled this era in Ferguson and recounted that African Americans knew that, for them, the City was "off-limits."

The Ferguson of half a century ago is not the same Ferguson that exists today. We heard from many residents—black and white—who expressed pride in their community, especially with regard to the fact that Ferguson is one of the most demographically diverse communities in the area. Pride in this aspect of Ferguson is well founded; Ferguson is more diverse than most of the United States, and than many of its surrounding cities. It is clear that many Ferguson residents of different races genuinely embrace that diversity.

But we also found evidence during our investigation that some within Ferguson still have difficulty coming to terms with Ferguson's changing demographics and seeing Ferguson's African American and white residents as equals in civic life. While total population rates have remained relatively constant over the last three decades, the portion of Ferguson residents who are African American has increased steadily but dramatically, from 25% in 1990 to 67% in 2010. Some individuals, including individuals charged with discretionary enforcement decisions in either the police department or the court, have expressed concerns about the increasing number of African Americans that have moved to Ferguson in recent years. Similarly, some City officials and residents we spoke with explicitly distinguished Ferguson's African-American residents from Ferguson's "normal" residents or "regular" people. One white third-generation Ferguson resident told us that in many ways Ferguson is "progressive and quite vibrant," while in another it is "typical—trying to hang on to its 'whiteness.'"

On its own, Ferguson's historical backdrop as a racially segregated community that did not treat African Americans equally under the law does not demonstrate that law enforcement practices today are motivated by impermissible discriminatory intent. It is one factor to consider, however, especially given the evidence that, among some in Ferguson, these attitudes persist today. As courts have instructed, the historical background of an official practice that leads to discriminatory effects is, together with other evidence, probative as to whether that practice is grounded in part in discriminatory purposes. *See Vill. of Arlington Heights*, 429 U.S. at 267; *see also Rogers v. Lodge*, 458 U.S. 613, *passim* (1982).

e. Failure to Evaluate or Correct Practices that Have Long Resulted in a Racially Disparate Impact

That the discriminatory effect of Ferguson's law enforcement practices is the result of intentional discrimination is further evidenced by the fact that City, police, and court officials have consistently failed to evaluate or reform—and in fact appear to have redoubled their commitment to—the very practices that have plainly and consistently exerted a disparate impact on African Americans.

The disparities we have identified appear to be longstanding. The statistical analysis performed as part of our investigation relied upon police and court data from recent years, but FPD has collected data related to vehicle stops pursuant to state requirements since 2000. Each year, that information is gathered by FPD, sent to the office of the Missouri Attorney General, and published on the Missouri Attorney General's webpage.[52] The data show disparate impact on African Americans in Ferguson for as long as that data has been reported. Based on that racial profiling data, Missouri publishes a "Disparity Index" for each reporting municipality, calculated as the percent of stops of a certain racial group compared with that group's local population rate. In each of the last 14 years, the data show that African Americans are "over represented" in FPD's vehicular stops.[53] That data also shows that in most years, FPD officers searched African Americans at higher rates than others, but found contraband on African Americans at lower rates.

In 2001, for example, African Americans comprised about the same proportion of the population as whites, but while stops of white drivers accounted for 1,495 stops, African Americans accounted for 3,426, more than twice as many. While a white person stopped that year was searched in 6% of cases, a black person stopped was searched in 14% of cases. That same year, searches of whites resulted in a contraband finding in 21% of cases, but searches of African Americans only resulted in a contraband finding in 16% of cases. Similar disparities were identified in most other years, with varying degrees of magnitude. In any event, the data reveals a pattern of racial disparities in Ferguson's police activities. That pattern appears to have been ignored by Ferguson officials.

That the extant racial disparities are intentional is also evident in the fact that Ferguson has consistently returned to the unlawful practices described in Parts III.A. and B. of this Report knowing that they impose a persistent disparate impact on African Americans. City officials have continued to encourage FPD to stop and cite aggressively as part of its revenue generation efforts, even though that encouragement and increased officer discretion has yielded disproportionate African-American representation in FPD stops and citations. Until we recommended it during our investigation, FPD officials had not restricted officer discretion to issue multiple citations at once, even though the application of that discretion has led officers to issue far more citations to African Americans at once than others, on average, and even though only black individuals (35 in total) ever received five or more citations at once over a three-year period. FPD has not provided further guidance to constrain officer discretion in conducting searches, even though FPD officers have, for years, searched African Americans at higher rates than others but found contraband during those searches less often than in searches of individuals of other races.

Similarly, City officials have not taken any meaningful steps to contain the discretion of court clerks to grant continuances, clear warrants, or enable driver's license suspensions to be lifted, even though those practices have resulted in warrants being issued and executed at highly disproportionate rates against African Americans. Indeed, until the City of Ferguson repealed the Failure to Appear statute in September 2014—after this investigation began—the City had not taken meaningful steps to evaluate or reform any of the court practices described in this Report, even though the implementation of those practices has plainly exerted a disparate impact on African Americans.

FPD also has not significantly altered its use-of-force tactics, even though FPD records make clear that current force decisions disparately impact black suspects, and that officers appear to assess threat differently depending upon the race of the suspect. FPD, for example, has not reviewed or revised its canine program, even though available records show that canine officers have exclusively set their dogs against black individuals, often in cases where doing so was not justified by the danger presented. In many incidents in which officers used significant levels of force, the facts as described by the officers themselves did not appear to support the force used, especially in light of the fact that less severe tactics likely would have been equally effective. In some of these incidents, law enforcement experts with whom we consulted could find no explanation other than race to explain the severe tactics used.

During our investigation, FPD officials told us that their police tactics are responsive to the scenario at hand. But records suggest that, where a suspect or group of suspects is white, FPD applies a different calculus, typically resulting in a more measured law enforcement response. In one 2012 incident, for example, officers reported responding to a fight in progress at a local bar that involved white suspects. Officers reported encountering "40–50 people actively fighting, throwing bottles and glasses, as well as chairs." The report noted that "one subject had his ear bitten off." While the responding officers reported using force, they only used "minimal baton and flashlight strikes as well as fists, muscling techniques and knee strikes." While the report states that "due to the amount of subjects fighting, no physical arrests were possible," it notes also that four subjects were brought to the station for "safekeeping." While we have found other evidence that FPD later issued a wanted for two individuals as a result of the incident, FPD's response stands in stark contrast to the actions officers describe taking in many incidents involving black suspects, some of which we earlier described.

Based on this evidence, it is apparent that FPD requires better train-ing, limits on officer discretion, increased supervision, and more robust accountability systems, not only to ensure that officers act in accordance with the Fourth Amendment, but with the Fourteenth Amendment as well. FPD has failed to take any such corrective action, and instead has actively endorsed and encouraged the perpetuation of the practices that have led to such stark disparities. This, together with the totality of the facts that we have found, evidences that those practices exist, at least in part, on account of an unconstitutional discriminatory purpose. *See Feeney*, 442 U.S. at 279 n.24 (noting that the discriminatory intent inquiry is "practical," because what "any official entity is 'up to' may be plain from the results its actions achieve, or the results they avoid").

D. Ferguson Law Enforcement Practices Erode Community Trust, Especially Among Ferguson's African-American Residents, and Make Policing Less Effective, More Difficult, and Less Safe

The unlawful police misconduct and court practices described above have generated great distrust of Ferguson law enforcement, especially among African Americans.[54] As described below, other FPD practices further contribute to distrust, including FPD's failure to hold officers accountable for misconduct, failure to implement community policing principles, and the lack of diversity within FPD. Together, these practices severely dam-aged the relationship between African Americans and the Ferguson Police Department long before Michael Brown's shooting death in August 2014. This divide has made policing in Ferguson less effective, more difficult, and more likely to discriminate.

1. FERGUSON'S UNLAWFUL POLICE AND COURT PRACTICES HAVE LED TO DISTRUST AND RESENTMENT AMONG MANY IN FERGUSON

The lack of trust between a significant portion of Ferguson's residents, espe-cially its African-American residents, and the Ferguson Police Department has become, since August 2014, undeniable. The causes of this distrust and division, however, have been the subject of debate. City and police officials, and some other Ferguson residents, have asserted that this lack of meaningful connection with much of Ferguson's African-American community is due to the fact that they are "transient" renters; that they do not appreciate how much the City of Ferguson does for them; that "pop-culture" portrays alienating themes; or because of "rumors" that the police and municipal court are unyielding because they are driven by raising revenue.

Our investigation showed that the disconnect and distrust between much of Ferguson's African-American community and FPD is caused largely by years of the unlawful and unfair law enforcement practices by Ferguson's police department and municipal court described above. In the documents we reviewed, the meetings we observed and participated in, and in the hundreds of conversations Civil Rights Division staff had with residents of Ferguson and the surrounding area, many residents, primarily African-American residents, described being belittled, disbelieved, and treated with little regard for their legal rights by the Ferguson Police Department. One white individual who has lived in Ferguson for 48 years told us that it feels like Ferguson's police and court system is "designed to bring a black man down . . . [there are] no second chances." We heard from African-American residents who told us of Ferguson's "long history of targeting blacks for harassment and degrading treatment," and who described the steps they take to avoid this—from taking routes to work that skirt Ferguson to moving out of state. An African-American minister of a church in a nearby community told us that he doesn't allow his two sons to drive through Ferguson out of "fear that they will be targeted for arrest."

African Americans' views of FPD are shaped not just by *what* FPD officers do, but by *how* they do it. During our investigation, dozens of African Americans in Ferguson told us of verbal abuse by FPD officers during routine interactions, and these accounts are consistent with complaints people have made about FPD for years. In December 2011, for example, an African-American man alleged that as he was standing outside of Wal-Mart, an officer called him a "stupid motherf****r" and a "bastard."

According to the man, a lieutenant was on the scene and did nothing to re-proach the officer, instead threatening to arrest the man. In April 2012, offi-cers allegedly called an African-American woman a "bitch" and a "mental case" at the jail following an arrest. In June 2011, a 60-year-old man com-plained that an officer verbally harassed him while he stood in line to see the judge in municipal court. According to the man, the officer repeatedly ordered him to move forward as the line advanced and, because he did not advance far enough, turned to the other court-goers and joked, "he is hooked on phonics."

Another concern we heard from many African-American residents, and saw in the files we reviewed, was of casual intimidation by FPD officers, including threats to draw or fire their weapons, often for seemingly little or no cause. In September 2012, a 28-year resident of Ferguson complained to FPD about a traffic stop during which a lieutenant approached with a loud and confrontational manner with his hand on his holstered gun. The resident, who had a military police background, noted that the lieutenant's behavior, especially having his hand on his gun, ratcheted up the tension level, and he questioned why the lieutenant had been so aggressive. In an-other incident captured on video and discussed below in more detail, an of-ficer placed his gun on a wall or post and pointed it back and forth to each of two store employees as he talked to them while they took the trash out late one night. In another case discussed above, a person reported that an FPD officer removed his ECW during a traffic stop and continuously tapped the ECW on the roof of the person's car. These written complaints reported to FPD are consistent with complaints we heard from community members during our investigation about officers casually threatening to hurt or even shoot them.

It appears that many police and City officials were unaware of this dis-trust and fear of Ferguson police among African Americans prior to August 2014. Ferguson's Chief, for example, told us that prior to the Michael Brown shooting he thought community-police relations were good. During our investigation, however, City and police leadership, and many officers of all ranks, acknowledged a deep divide between police and some Ferguson residents, particularly black residents. Mayor Knowles acknowledged that there is "clearly mistrust" of FPD by many community members, including a "systemic problem" with youth not wanting to work with police. One FPD officer estimated that about a quarter of the Ferguson community distrusts the police department.

A growing body of research, alongside decades of police experience, is consistent with what our investigation found in Ferguson: that when police and courts treat people unfairly, unlawfully, or disrespectfully, law enforcement loses legitimacy in the eyes of those who have experienced, or even observed, the unjust conduct. *See, e.g.*, Tom R. Tyler & Yuen J. Huo, *Trust in the Law: Encouraging Public Cooperation with the Police and Courts* (2002). Further, this loss of legitimacy makes individuals more likely to resist enforcement efforts and less likely to cooperate with law enforcement efforts to prevent and investigate crime. *See, e.g.*, Jason Sunshine & Tom R. Tyler, *The Role of Procedural Justice and Legitimacy in Shaping Public Support for Policing*, 37 Law & Soc'y Rev. 513, 534–36 (2003); *Promoting Cooperative Strategies to Reduce Racial Profiling* 20–21 (U.S. Dep't of Justice, Office of Community Oriented Policing Services, 2008) ("Being viewed as fair and just is critical to successful policing in a democracy. When the police are perceived as unfair in their enforcement, it will undermine their effectiveness."); Ron Davis et al., *Exploring the Role of the Police in Prisoner Reentry* 13–14 (Nat'l Inst. of Justice, New Perspectives in Policing, July 2012) ("Increasingly, research is supporting the notion that legitimacy is an important factor in the effectiveness of law, and the establishment and maintenance of legitimacy are particularly important in the context of policing.") (citations omitted). To improve community trust and police effectiveness, Ferguson must ensure not only that its officers act in accord with the Constitution, but that they treat people fairly and respectfully.

2. FPD'S EXERCISE OF DISCRETION, EVEN WHEN LAWFUL, OFTEN UNDERMINES COMMUNITY TRUST AND PUBLIC SAFETY

Even where lawful, many discretionary FPD enforcement actions increase distrust and significantly decrease the likelihood that individuals will seek police assistance even when they are victims of crime, or that they will cooperate with the police to solve or prevent other crimes. Chief Jackson told us "we don't get cooperating witnesses" from the apartment complexes. Consistent with this statement, our review of documents and our conversations with Ferguson residents revealed many instances in which they are reluctant to report being victims of crime or to cooperate with police, and many instances in which FPD imposed unnecessary negative consequences for doing so.

In one instance, for example, a woman called FPD to report a domestic disturbance. By the time the police arrived, the woman's boyfriend had left. The police looked through the house and saw indications that the boyfriend lived there. When the woman told police that only she and her brother were listed on the home's occupancy permit, the officer placed the woman under arrest for the permit violation and she was jailed. In another instance, after a woman called police to report a domestic disturbance and was given a summons for an occupancy permit violation, she said, according to the officer's report, that she "hated the Ferguson Police Department and will never call again, even if she is being killed."

In another incident, a young African-American man was shot while walking on the road with three friends. The police department located and interviewed two of the friends about the shooting. After the interview, they arrested and jailed one of these cooperating witnesses, who was 19 years old, on an outstanding municipal warrant.

We also reviewed many instances in which FPD officers arrested individuals who sought to care for loved ones who had been hurt. In one instance from May 2014, for example, a man rushed to the scene of a car accident involving his girlfriend, who was badly injured and bleeding profusely when he arrived. He approached and tried to calm her. When officers arrived they treated him rudely, according to the man, telling him to move away from his girlfriend, which he did not want to do. They then immediately proceeded to handcuff and arrest him, which, officers assert, he resisted. EMS and other officers were not on the scene during this arrest, so the accident victim remained unattended, bleeding from her injuries, while officers were arresting the boyfriend. Officers charged the man with five municipal code violations (Resisting Arrest, Disorderly Conduct, Assault on an Officer, Obstructing Government Operations, and Failure to Comply) and had his vehicle towed and impounded. In an incident from 2013, a woman sought to reach her fiancé, who was in a car accident. After she refused to stay on the sidewalk as the officer ordered, she was arrested and jailed. While it is sometimes both essential and difficult to keep distraught family from being in close proximity to their loved ones on the scene of an accident, there is rarely a need to arrest and jail them rather than, at most, detain them on the scene.

Rather than view these instances as opportunities to convey their compassion for individuals at times of crisis even as they maintain order, FPD appears instead to view these and similar incidents we reviewed as opportunities to issue multiple citations and make arrests. For very little public safety benefit, FPD loses opportunities to build community trust and respect, and instead further alienates potential allies in crime prevention.

3. FPD'S FAILURE TO RESPOND TO COMPLAINTS OF OFFICER MISCONDUCT FURTHER ERODES COMMUNITY TRUST

Public trust has been further eroded by FPD's lack of any meaningful system for holding officers accountable when they violate law or policy. Through its system for taking, investigating, and responding to misconduct complaints, a police department has the opportunity to demonstrate that officer misconduct is unacceptable and unrepresentative of how the law enforcement agency values and treats its constituents. In this way, a police department's internal affairs process provides an opportunity for the department to restore trust and affirm its legitimacy. Similarly, misconduct investigations allow law enforcement the opportunity to provide community members who have been mistreated a constructive, effective way to voice their complaints. And, of course, effective internal affairs processes can be a critical part of correcting officer behavior, and improving police training and policies.

Ferguson's internal affairs system fails to respond meaningfully to complaints of officer misconduct. It does not serve as a mechanism to re-store community members' trust in law enforcement, or correct officer be-havior. Instead, it serves to contrast FPD's tolerance for officer misconduct against the Department's aggressive enforcement of even minor municipal infractions, lending credence to a sentiment that we heard often from Fer-guson residents: that a "different set of rules" applies to Ferguson's police than to its African-American residents, and that making a complaint about officer misconduct is futile.

Despite the statement in FPD's employee misconduct investigation pol-icy that "[t]he integrity of the police department depends on the personal integrity and discipline of each employee," FPD has done little to investi-gate external allegations that officers have not followed FPD policy or the law, or, with a few notable exceptions, to hold officers accountable when they have not. Ferguson Police Department makes it difficult to make com-plaints about officer conduct, and frequently assumes that the officer is tell-ing the truth and the complainant is not, even where objective evidence indicates that the reverse is true.

It is difficult for individuals to make a misconduct complaint against an officer in Ferguson, in part because Ferguson both discourages individu-als from making complaints and discourages City and police staff from ac-cepting them. In a March 2014 email, for example, a lieutenant criticized a sergeant for taking a complaint from a man on behalf of his mother, who stayed in her vehicle outside the police station. Despite the fact that Fergu-son policy requires that complaints be taken "from any source, identified or anonymous," the lieutenant stated "I would have had him bring her in, or leave." In another instance, a City employee took a complaint of miscon-duct from a Ferguson resident and relayed it to FPD. An FPD captain sent an email in response that the City employee viewed as being "lectured" for taking the complaint. The City Manager agreed, calling the captain's behavior "not only disrespectful and unacceptable, but it is dangerous in [that] it is inciteful [sic] and divisive." Nonetheless, there appeared to be no follow-up action regarding the captain, and the complaint was never logged as such or investigated.

While official FPD policy states clearly that officers must "never attempt to dissuade any citizen from lodging a complaint," FPD General Order 301.3, a contrary leadership message speaks louder than policy. This message is reflected in statements by officers that indicate a need to justify their actions when they do accept a civilian complaint. In one case, a sergeant explained: "Nothing I could say helped, he demanded the complaint forms which were provided." In another: "I spoke to [two people seeking to make a complaint] . . . but after the conversation, neither had changed their mind and desired still to write out a complaint." We saw many instances in which people complained of being prevented from making a complaint, with no indication that FPD investigated those allegations. In one instance, for example, a man alleging significant excessive force reported the incident to a commander after being released from jail, stating that he was unable to make his complaint earlier because several different officers refused to let him speak to a sergeant to make a complaint about the incident and threatened to keep him in jail longer if he did not stop asking to make a complaint.

Some individuals also fear that they will suffer retaliation from officers if they report misconduct or even merely speak out as witnesses when approached by someone from FPD investigating a misconduct complaint. For instance, in one case FPD acknowledged that a witness to the misconduct was initially reluctant to complete a written statement supporting the complainant because he wanted no "repercussions" from the subject officer or other officers. In another case involving alleged misconduct at a retail store that we have already described, the store's district manager told the commander he did not want an investigation—despite how concerned he was by video footage showing an officer training his gun on two store employees as they took out the trash—because he wanted to "stay on the good side" of the police.

Even when individuals do report misconduct, there is a significant likelihood it will not be treated as a complaint and investigated. In one case, FPD failed to open an investigation of an allegation made by a caller who said an officer had kicked him in the side of the head and stepped on his head and back while he was face down with his hands cuffed behind his back, all the while talking about having blood on him from somebody else and "being tired of the B.S." The officer did not stop until the other officer on the scene said words to the effect of, "[h]ey, he's not fighting he's cuffed." The man alleged that the officer then ordered him to "get the f*** up" and lifted him by the handcuffs, yanking his arms backward. The commander taking the call reported that the man stated that he supported the police and knew they had a tough job but was reporting the incident because it appeared the officer was under a lot of stress and needed counseling, and because he was hoping to prevent others from having the experience he did. The commander's email regarding the incident expressed no skepticism about the veracity of the caller's report and was able to identify the incident (and thus the involved officers). Yet FPD did not conduct an internal affairs investigation of this incident, based on our review of all of FPD's internal investigation files. There is not even an indication that a use-of-force report was completed.

In another case, an FPD commander wrote to a sergeant that despite a complainant being "pretty adamant that she was profiled and that the officer was rude," the commander "didn't even bother to send it to the chief for a control number" before hearing the sergeant's account of the officer's side of the story. Upon getting the officer's account second hand from the sergeant, the commander forwarded the information to the Police Chief so that it could be "filed in the non-complaint file." FPD officers and commanders also often seek to frame complaints as being entirely related to complainants' guilt or innocence, and therefore not subject to a misconduct investigation, even though the complaint clearly alleges officer misconduct. In one instance, for example, commanders told the complainant to go to court to fight her arrest, ignoring the complainant's statement that the officer arrested her for Disorderly Conduct and Failure to Obey only after she asked for the officer's name. In another instance, a commander stated that the complainant made no allegations unrelated to the merits of the arrest, even though the complainant alleged rudeness and being "intimidated" during arrest, among a number of other non-guilt related allegations.

FPD appears to intentionally *not* treat allegations of misconduct as complaints even where it believes that the officer in fact committed the misconduct. In one incident, for example, a supervisor wrote an email directly to an officer about a complaint the Police Chief had received about an officer speeding through the park in a neighboring town. The supervisor informed the officer that the Chief tracked the car number given by the complainant back to the officer, but assured the officer that the supervisor's email was "[j]ust for your information. No need to reply and there is no record of this other than this email." In another instance referenced above, the district manager of a retail store called a commander to tell him that he had a video recording that showed an FPD officer pull up to the store at about midnight while two employees were taking out the trash, take out his weapon, and put it on top of a concrete wall, pointed at the two employees. When the employees said they were just taking out the trash and asked the officer if he needed them to take off their coats so that he could see their uniforms, the officer told the employees that he knew they were employees and that if he had not known "I would have put you on the ground." The commander related in an email to the sergeant and lieutenant that "there is no reason to doubt the Gen. Manager because he said he watched the video and he clearly saw a weapon—maybe the sidearm or the taser." Nonetheless, despite noting that "we don't need cowboy" and the "major concern" of the officer taking his weapon out of his holster and placing it on a wall, the commander concluded, "[n]othing for you to do with this other than make a mental note and for you to be on the lookout for that kind of behavior."[55]

In another case, an officer investigating a report of a theft at a dollar store interrogated a minister pumping gas into his church van about the theft. The man alleged that he provided his identification to the officer and offered to return to the store to prove he was not the thief. The officer instead handcuffed the man and drove him to the store. The store clerk reported that the detained man was not the thief, but the officer continued to keep the man cuffed, allegedly calling him "f*****g stupid" for asking to be released from the cuffs. The man went directly to FPD to file a complaint upon being released by the officer. FPD conducted an investigation but, because the complainant did not respond to a cell phone message left by the investigator within 13 days, reclassified the complaint as "withdrawn," even as the investigator noted that the complaint of improper detention would otherwise have been sustained, and noted that the "[e]mployee has been counseled and retraining is forthcoming." In still another case, a lieutenant of a neighboring agency called FPD to report that a pizza parlor owner had complained to him that an off-duty FPD officer had become angry upon being told that police discounts were only given to officers in uniform and said to the restaurant owner as he was leaving, "I hope you get robbed!" The allegation was not considered a complaint and instead, despite its seriousness, was handled through counseling at the squad level.[56]

Even where a complaint is actually investigated, unless the complaint is made by an FPD commander, and sometimes not even then, FPD consistently takes the word of the officer over the word of the complainant, frequently even where the officer's version of events is clearly at odds with the objective evidence. On the rare occasion that FPD does sustain an external complaint of officer misconduct, the discipline it imposes is generally too low to be an effective deterrent.[57]

Our investigation raised concerns in particular about how FPD responds to untruthfulness by officers. In many departments, a finding of untruthfulness pursuant to internal investigation results in an officer's termination because the officer's credibility on police reports and in providing testimony is subsequently subject to challenge. In FPD, untruthfulness appears not even to always result in a formal investigation, and even where sustained, has little effect. In one case we reviewed, FPD sustained a charge of untruthfulness against an officer after he was found to have lied to the investigator about whether he had engaged in an argument with a civilian over the loudspeaker of his police vehicle. FPD imposed only a 12-hour suspension on the officer. In addition, FPD appears not to have taken the officer's untruthfulness into sufficient account in several subsequent complaints, including in at least one case in which the complainant alleged conduct very similar to that alleged in the case in which FPD found the officer untruthful. Nor, as discussed above, has FPD or the City disclosed this information to defendants challenging charges brought by the officer. In another case a supervisor was sustained for false testimony during an internal affairs investigation and was given a written reprimand. In another case in which an officer was clearly untruthful, FPD did not sustain the charge.[58] In that case, an officer in another jurisdiction was assigned to monitor an intersection in that city because an FPD-marked vehicle allegedly had repeatedly been running the stop sign at that intersection. While at that intersection, and while receiving a complaint from a person about the FPD vehicle, the officer saw that very vehicle "dr[iving] through the stop sign without tapping a brake," according to a sergeant with the other jurisdiction. When asked to respond to these allegations, the officer wrote, unequivocally, "I assure you I don't run stop signs." It is clear from the investigative file that FPD found that he did, in fact, run stop signs, as the officer was given counseling. Nonetheless, the officer received a counseling memo that made no mention of the officer's written denial of the misconduct observed by another law enforcement officer. This officer continues to write reports regarding significant uses of force, several of which our investigation found questionable.[59]

By failing to hold officers accountable, FPD leadership sends a message that FPD officers can behave as they like, regardless of law or policy, and even if caught, that punishment will be light. This message serves to condone officer misconduct and fuel community distrust.

4. FPD'S LACK OF COMMUNITY ENGAGEMENT INCREASES THE LIKELIHOOD OF DISCRIMINATORY POLICING AND DAMAGES PUBLIC TRUST

Alongside its divisive law enforcement practices and lack of meaningful response to community concerns about police conduct, FPD has made little effort in recent years to employ community policing or other community engagement strategies. This lack of community engagement has precluded the possibility of bridging the divide caused by Ferguson's law enforcement practices, and has increased the likelihood of discriminatory policing.

Community policing and related community engagement strategies provide the opportunity for officers and communities to work together to identify the causes of crime and disorder particular to their community, and to prioritize law enforcement efforts. *See Community Policing Defined* 1-16 (U.S. Dep't of Justice, Office of Community Oriented Policing Services, 2014). The focus of these strategies—in stark contrast to Ferguson's current law enforcement approach—is on crime prevention rather than on making arrests. *See Effective Policing and Crime Prevention: A Problem Oriented Guide for Mayors, City Managers, and County Executives* 1-62 (U.S. Dep't of Justice, Office of Community Oriented Policing Services, 2009). When implemented fully, community policing creates opportunities for officers and community members to have frequent, positive interactions with each other, and requires officers to partner with communities to solve particular public safety problems that, together, they have decided to address. Research and experience show that community policing can be more effective at crime prevention and at making people feel safer. *See* Gary Cordner, *Reducing Fear of Crime: Strategies for Police* 47 (U.S. Dep't of Justice, Office of Community Oriented Policing Services, Jan. 2010) ("Most studies of community policing have found that residents like community policing and feel safer when it is implemented where they live and work.") (citations omitted).

Further, research and law enforcement experience show that community policing and engagement can overcome many of the divisive dynamics that disconnected Ferguson residents and City leadership alike describe, from a dearth of positive interactions to racial stereotyping and racial violence. *See, e.g.*, Glaser, *supra*, at 207-11 (discussing research showing that community policing and similar approaches can help reduce racial bias and stereotypes and improve community relations); L. Song Richardson &

Phillip Atiba Goff, *Interrogating Racial Violence*, 12 Ohio St. J. of Crim. L. 115, 143–47 (2014) (describing how fully implemented and inclusive community policing can help avoid racial stereotyping and violence); *Strengthening the Relationship Between Law Enforcement and Communities of Color: Developing an Agenda for Action* 1–20 (U.S. Dep't of Justice, Office of Community Oriented Policing Services, 2014).

Ferguson's community policing efforts appear always to have been somewhat modest, but have dwindled to almost nothing in recent years. FPD has no community policing or community engagement plan. FPD currently designates a single officer the "Community Resource Officer." This officer attends community meetings, serves as FPD's public relations liaison, and is charged with collecting crime data. No other officers play any substantive role in community policing efforts. Officers we spoke with were fairly consistent in their acknowledgment of this, and of the fact that this move away from community policing has been due, at least in part, to an increased focus on code enforcement and revenue generation in recent years. As discussed above, our investigation found that FPD redeployed officers to 12-hour shifts, in part for revenue reasons. There is some evidence that community policing is more difficult to carry out when patrol officers are on 12-hour shifts, and this appears to be the case in Ferguson. While many officers in Ferguson support 12-hour shifts, several told us that the 12- hour shift has undermined community policing. One officer said that "FPD used to have a strong community policing ethic—then we went to a 12-hour day." Another officer told us that the 12- hour schedule, combined with a lack of any attempt to have officers remain within their assigned area, has resulted in a lack of any geographical familiarity by FPD officers. This same officer told us that it is viewed as more positive to write tickets than to "talk with your businesses." Another officer told us that FPD officers should put less energy into writing tickets and instead "get out of their cars" and get to know community members.

One officer told us that officers could spend more time engaging with community members and undertaking problem-solving projects if FPD officers were not so focused on activities that generate revenue. This officer told us, "everything's about the courts . . . the court's enforcement priorities are money." Another officer told us that officers cannot "get out of the car and play basketball with the kids," because "we've removed all the basketball hoops—there's an ordinance against it." While one officer told us that there was a police substation in Canfield Green when FPD was more committed to community policing, another told us that now there is "nobody in there that anybody knows."

City and police officials note that there are several active neighborhood groups in Ferguson. We reached out to each of these during our investigation and met with each one that responded. Some areas of Ferguson are well-represented by these groups. But City and police officials acknowledge that, since August 2014, they have realized that there are entire segments of the Ferguson community that they have never made an effort to know, especially African Americans who live in Ferguson's large apartment complexes, including Canfield Green. While some City officials appear well-intentioned, they have also been too quick to presume that outreach to more disconnected segments of the Ferguson community will be futile. One City employee told us, "they think they do outreach, but they don't," and that some Ferguson residents do not even realize their homes are in Ferguson. Our investigation indicated that, while the City and police department may have to use different strategies for engagement in some parts of Ferguson than in others, true community policing efforts can have positive results. As an officer who has patrolled the area told us, "most of the people in Canfield are good people. They just don't have a lot of time to get involved."

5. FERGUSON'S LACK OF A DIVERSE POLICE FORCE FURTHER UNDERMINES COMMUNITY TRUST

While approximately two-thirds of Ferguson's residents are African American, only four of Ferguson's 54 commissioned police officers are African American. Since August 2014, there has been widespread discussion about the impact this comparative lack of racial diversity within FPD has on community trust and police behavior. During this investigation we also heard repeated complaints about FPD's lack of racial diversity from members of the Ferguson community. Our investigation indicates that greater diversity within Ferguson Police Department has the potential to increase community confidence in the police department, but may only be successful as part of a broader police reform effort.

While it does appear that a lack of racial diversity among officers decreases African Americans' trust in a police department, this observation must be qualified. Increasing a police department's racial diversity does not necessarily increase community trust or improve officer conduct. There appear to be many reasons for this. One important reason is that African-American officers can abuse and violate the rights of African-American civilians, just as white officers can. And African-American officers who behave abusively can undermine community trust just as white officers can. Our investigation indicates that in Ferguson, individual officer behavior is largely driven by a police culture that focuses on revenue generation and is infected by race bias. While increased vertical and horizontal diversity, racial and otherwise, likely is necessary to change this culture, it probably cannot do so on its own.

Consistent with our findings in Ferguson and other departments, research more broadly shows that a racially diverse police force does not guarantee community trust or lawful policing. *See Diversity in Law Enforcement: A Literature Review* 4 n.v. (U.S. Dep't of Justice, Civil Rights Division, Office of Justice Programs, & U.S. Equal Employment Opportunity Commission, Submission to President's Task Force on 21st Century Policing, Jan. 2015). The picture is far more complex. Some studies show that Africa-American officers are less prejudiced than white officers as a whole, are more familiar with African-American communities, are more likely to arrest white suspects and less likely to arrest black suspects, and receive more cooperation from African Americans with whom they interact on the job. *See* David A. Sklansky, *Not Your Father's Police Department:*

Making Sense of the New Demographics of Law Enforcement, 96 J. Crim. L. & Criminology 1209, 1224–25 (2006). But studies also show that African Americans are equally likely to fire their weapons, arrest people, and have complaints made about their behavior, and sometimes harbor prejudice against African-American civilians themselves. *Id.*

While a diverse police department does not guarantee a constitutional one, it is nonetheless critically important for law enforcement agencies, and the Ferguson Police Department in particular, to strive for broad diversity among officers and civilian staff. In general, notwithstanding the above caveats, a more racially diverse police department has the potential to increase confidence in police among African Americans in particular. *See* Joshua C. Cochran & Patricia Y. Warren, *Racial, Ethnic, and Gender Differences in, Perceptions of the Police: The Salience of Officer Race Within the Context of Racial Profiling*, 28(2) J. Contemp. Crim. Just. 206, 206–27 (2012). In addition, diversity of all types—including race, ethnicity, sex, national origin, religion, sexual orientation and gender identity—can be beneficial both to police-community relationships and the culture of the law enforcement agency. Increasing gender and sexual orientation diversity in policing in particular may be critical in re-making internal police culture and creating new assumptions about what makes policing effective. *See, e.g.*, Sklansky, *supra*, at 1233–34; Richardson & Goff, *supra*, at 143–47; Susan L. Miller, Kay B. Forest, & Nancy C. Jurik, *Diversity in Blue, Lesbian and Gay Police Officers in a Masculine Occupation*, 5 Men and Masculinities 355, 355–85 (Apr. 2003).[60] Moreover, aside from the beneficial impact a diverse police force may have on the culture of the department and police-community relations, police departments are obligated under law to provide equal opportunity for employment. *See* Title VII of the Civil Rights Act of 1964, 42 U.S.C. § 2000e *et seq.*

Our investigation indicates that Ferguson can and should do more to attract and hire a more diverse group of qualified police officers.[61] However, for these efforts to be successful at increasing the diversity of its workforce, as well as effective at increasing community trust and improving officer behavior, they must be part of a broader reform effort within FPD. This reform effort must focus recruitment efforts on attracting qualified candidates of *all* demographics with the skills and temperament to police respectfully and effectively, and must ensure that *all* officers—regardless of race—are required to police lawfully and with integrity.

V. CHANGES NECESSARY TO REMEDY FERGUSON'S UNLAWFUL LAW ENFORCEMENT PRACTICES AND REPAIR COMMUNITY TRUST

THE PROBLEMS IDENTIFIED WITHIN THIS LETTER REFLECT DEEPLY entrenched practices and priorities that are incompatible with lawful and effective policing and that damage community trust. Addressing those problems and repairing the City's relationship with the community will require a fundamental redirection of Ferguson's approach to law enforcement, including the police and court practices that reflect and perpetuate this approach.

Below we set out broad recommendations for changes that Ferguson should make to its police and court practices to correct the constitutional violations our investigation identified. Ensuring meaningful, sustainable, and verifiable reform will require that these and other measures be part of a court-enforceable remedial process that includes involvement from community stakeholders as well as independent oversight. In the coming weeks, we will seek to work with the City of Ferguson toward developing and reaching agreement on an appropriate framework for reform.

A. Ferguson Police Practices

1. **IMPLEMENT A ROBUST SYSTEM OF TRUE COMMUNITY POLICING**

Many of the recommendations included below would require a shift from policing to raise revenue to policing in partnership with the entire Ferguson community. Developing these relationships will take time and considerable effort. FPD should:

a. Develop and put into action a policy and detailed plan for comprehensive implementation of community policing and problem-solving principles. Conduct outreach and involve the entire community in developing and implementing this plan;

b. Increase opportunities for officers to have frequent, positive interactions with people outside of an enforcement context, especially groups that have expressed high levels of distrust of police. Such opportunities may include police athletic leagues and similar informal activities;

c. Develop community partnerships to identify crime prevention priorities, with a focus on disconnected areas, such as Ferguson's apartment complexes, and disconnected groups, such as much of Ferguson's African-American youth;

d. Modify officer deployment patterns and scheduling (such as moving away from the current 12-hour shift and assigning officers to patrol the same geographic areas consistently) to facilitate participating in crime prevention projects and familiarity with areas and people;

e. Train officers on crime-prevention, officer safety, and anti-discrimination advantages of community policing. Train officers on mechanics of community policing and their role in implementing it;

f. Measure and evaluate individual, supervisory, and agency police performance on community engagement, problem-oriented-policing projects, and crime prevention, rather than on arrest and citation productivity.

2. FOCUS STOP, SEARCH, TICKETING AND ARREST PRACTICES ON COMMUNITY PROTECTION

FPD must fundamentally change the way it conducts stops and searches, issues citations and summonses, and makes arrests. FPD officers must be trained and required to abide by the law. In addition, FPD enforcement efforts should be reoriented so that officers are required to take enforcement action because it promotes public safety, not simply because they have legal authority to act. To do this, FPD should:

a. Prohibit the use of ticketing and arrest quotas, whether formal or informal;

b. Require that officers report in writing all stops, searches and arrests, including pedestrian stops, and that their reports articulate the legal authority for the law enforcement action and sufficient description of facts to support that authority;

c. Require documented supervisory approval prior to:

1) Issuing any citation/summons that includes more than two charges;

2) Making an arrest on any of the following charges:

   i. Failure to Comply/Obey;

   ii. Resisting Arrest;

   iii. Disorderly Conduct/Disturbing the Peace

   iv. Obstruction of Government Operations;

3) Arresting or ticketing an individual who sought police aid, or who is cooperating with police in an investigation;

4) Arresting on a municipal warrant or wanted;

d. Revise Failure to Comply municipal code provision to bring within constitutional limits, and provide sufficient guidance so that all stops, citations, and arrests based on the provision comply with the Constitution;

e. Train officers on proper use of Failure to Comply charge, including elements of the offense and appropriateness of the charge for interference with police activity that threatens public safety;

f. Require that applicable legal standards are met before officers conduct pat-downs or vehicle searches. Prohibit searches based on consent for the foreseeable future;

g. Develop system of correctable violation, or "fix-it" tickets, and require officers to issue fix-it tickets wherever possible and absent contrary supervisory instruction;

h. Develop and implement policy and training regarding appropriate police response to activities protected by the First Amendment, including the right to observe, record, and protest police action;

i. Provide initial and regularly recurring training on Fourth Amendment constraints on police action, as well as responsibility within FPD to constrain action beyond what Fourth Amendment requires in interest of public safety and community trust;

j. Discontinue use of "wanteds" or "stop orders" and prohibit officers from conducting stops, searches, or arrests on the basis of "wanteds" or "stop orders" issued by other agencies.

3. INCREASE TRACKING, REVIEW, AND ANALYSIS OF FPD STOP, SEARCH, TICKETING AND ARREST PRACTICES

At the first level of supervision and as an agency, FPD must review more stringently officers' stop, search, ticketing, and arrest practices to ensure that officers are complying with the 92 Constitution and department policy, and to evaluate the impact of officer activity on police legitimacy and community trust. FPD should:

a. Develop and implement a plan for broader collection of stop, search, ticketing, and arrest data that includes pedestrian stops, enhances vehicle stop data collection, and requires collection of data on all stop and post-stop activity, as well as location and demographic information;

b. Require supervisors to review all officer activity and review all officer reports before the supervisor leaves shift;

c. Develop and implement system for regular review of stop, search, ticketing, and arrest data at supervisory and agency

level to detect problematic trends and ensure consistency with
public safety and community policing goals;

d. Analyze race and other disparities shown in stop, search, ticketing, and arrest practices to determine whether disparities can be
reduced consistent with public safety goals.

4. CHANGE FORCE USE, REPORTING, REVIEW, AND RESPONSE TO ENCOURAGE DE-ESCALATION AND THE USE OF THE MINIMAL FORCE NECESSARY IN A SITUATION

FPD should reorient officers' approach to using force by ensuring that they
are trained and skilled in using tools and tactics to de-escalate situations,
and incentivized to avoid using force wherever possible. FPD also should
implement a system of force review that ensures that improper force is detected and responded to effectively, and that policy, training, tactics, and
officer safety concerns are identified. FPD should:

a. Train and require officers to use de-escalation techniques wherever possible both to avoid a situation escalating to where force
becomes necessary, and to avoid unnecessary force even where
it would be legally justified. Training should include tactics for
slowing down a situation to increase available options;

b. Require onsite supervisory approval before deploying any canine, absent documented exigent circumstances; require and
train canine officers to take into account the nature and severity of the alleged crime when deciding whether to deploy a canine to bite; require and train canine officers to avoid sending
a canine to apprehend by biting a concealed suspect when the
objective facts do not suggest the suspect is armed and a lower
level of force reasonably can be expected to secure the suspect;

c. Place more stringent limits on use of ECWs, including limitations on multiple ECW cycles and detailed justification for using more than one cycle;

d. Retrain officers in use of ECWs to ensure they view and use

ECWs as a tool of necessity, not convenience. Training should be consistent with principles set out in the *2011 ECW Guidelines*;

e. Develop and implement use-of-force reporting that requires the officer using force to complete a narrative, separate from the offense report, describing the force used with particularity, and describing with specificity the circumstances that required the level of force used, including the reason for the initial stop or other enforcement action. Some levels of force should require all officers observing the use of force to complete a separate force narrative;

f. Develop and implement supervisory review of force that requires the supervisor to conduct a complete review of each use of force, including gathering and considering evidence necessary to understand the circumstances of the force incident and determine its consistency with law and policy, including statements from individuals against whom force is used and civilian witnesses;

g. Prohibit supervisors from reviewing or investigating a use of force in which they participated or directed;

h. Ensure that complete use-of-force reporting and review/investigation files—including all offense reports, witness statements, and medical, audio/video, and other evidence—are kept together in a centralized location;

i. Develop and implement a system for higher-level, interdisciplinary review of some types of force, such as lethal force, canine deployment, ECWs, and force resulting in any injury;

j. Improve collection, review, and response to use-of-force data, including information regarding ECW and canine use;

k. Implement system of zero tolerance for use of force as punishment or retaliation rather than as necessary, proportionate response to counter a threat;

l. Discipline officers who fail to report force and supervisors who fail to conduct adequate force investigations;

m. Identify race and other disparities in officer use of force and develop strategies to eliminate avoidable disparities;

n. Staff jail with at least two correctional officers at all times to ensure safety and minimize need for use of force in dealing with intoxicated or combative prisoners. Train correctional officers in de-escalation techniques with specific instruction and training on minimizing force when dealing with intoxicated and combative prisoners, as well as with passive resistance and noncompliance.

5. IMPLEMENT POLICIES AND TRAINING TO IMPROVE INTERACTIONS WITH VULNERABLE PEOPLE

Providing officers with the tools and training to better respond to persons in physical or mental health crisis, and to those with intellectual disabilities, will help avoid unnecessary injuries, increase community trust, and make officers safer. FPD should:

a. Develop and implement policy and training for identifying and responding to individuals with known or suspected mental health conditions, including those observably in mental health crisis, and those with intellectual or other disabilities;

b. Provide enhanced crisis intervention training to a subset of officers to allow for ready availability of trained officers on the scenes of critical incidents involving individuals with mentally illness;

c. Require that, wherever possible, at least one officer with enhanced crisis intervention training respond to any situation concerning individuals in mental health crisis or with intellectual disability, when force might be used;

d. Provide training to officers regarding how to identify and respond to more commonly occurring medical emergencies that may at first appear to reflect a failure to comply with lawful orders. Such medical emergencies may include, for example, seizures and diabetic emergencies.

6. CHANGE RESPONSE TO STUDENTS TO AVOID CRIMINALIZING YOUTH WHILE MAINTAINING A LEARNING ENVIRONMENT

FPD has the opportunity to profoundly impact students through its SRO program. This program can be used as a way to build positive relationships with youth from a young age and to support strategies to keep students in school and learning. FPD should:

a. Work with school administrators, teachers, parents, and students to develop and implement policy and training consistent with law and best practices to more effectively address disciplinary issues in schools. This approach should be focused on SROs developing positive relationships with youth in support of maintaining a learning environment without unnecessarily treating disciplinary issues as criminal matters or resulting in the routine imposition of lengthy suspensions;

b. Provide initial and regularly recurring training to SROs, including training in mental health, counseling, and the development of the teenage brain;

c. Evaluate SRO performance on student engagement and prevention of disturbances, rather than on student arrests or removals;

d. Regularly review and evaluate incidents in which SROs are involved to ensure they meet the particular goals of the SRO program; to identify any disparate impact or treatment by race or other protected basis; and to identify any policy, training, or equipment concerns.

7. IMPLEMENT MEASURES TO REDUCE BIAS AND ITS IMPACT ON POLICE BEHAVIOR

Many of the recommendations listed elsewhere have the potential to reduce the level and impact of bias on police behavior (e.g., increasing positive interactions between police and the community; increasing the collection and analysis of stop data; and increasing oversight of the exercise of police discretion). Below are additional measures that can assist in this effort. FPD should:

a. Provide initial and recurring training to all officers that sends a clear, consistent and emphatic message that bias-based profiling and other forms of discriminatory policing are prohibited. Training should include:

   1) Relevant legal and ethical standards;
   2) Information on how stereotypes and implicit bias can infect police work;
   3) The importance of procedural justice and police legitimacy on community trust, police effectiveness, and officer safety;
   4) The negative impacts of profiling on public safety and crime prevention;

b. Provide training to supervisors and commanders on detecting and responding to bias-based profiling and other forms of discriminatory policing;

c. Include community members from groups that have expressed high levels of distrust of police in officer training;

d. Take steps to eliminate all forms of workplace bias from FPD and the City.

8. IMPROVE AND INCREASE TRAINING GENERALLY

FPD officers receive far too little training as recruits and after becoming officers. Officers need a better knowledge of what law, policy, and integrity require, and concrete training on how to carry out their police responsibilities. In addition to the training specified elsewhere in these recommendations, FPD should:

a. Significantly increase the quality and amount of all types of officer training, including recruit, field training (including for officers hired from other agencies), and in-service training;

b. Require that training cover, in depth, constitutional and other legal restrictions on officer action, as well as additional factors officers should consider before taking enforcement action (such as police legitimacy and procedural justice considerations);

c. Employ scenario-based and adult-learning methods.

9. INCREASE CIVILIAN INVOLVEMENT IN POLICE DECISION MAKING

In addition to engaging with all segments of Ferguson as part of implementing community policing, FPD should develop and implement a system that incorporates civilian input into all aspects of policing, including policy development, training, use-of-force review, and investigation of misconduct complaints.

10. IMPROVE OFFICER SUPERVISION

The recommendations set out here cannot be implemented without dedicated, skilled, and well-trained supervisors who police lawfully and without bias. FPD should:

a. Provide all supervisors with specific supervisory training prior to assigning them to supervisory positions;

b. Develop and require supervisors to use an "early intervention system" to objectively detect problematic patterns of officer misconduct, assist officers who need additional attention, and identify training and equipment needs;

c. Support supervisors who encourage and guide respectful policing and implement community policing principles, and evaluate them on this basis. Remove supervisors who do not adequately review officer activity and reports or fail to support, through words or actions, unbiased policing;

d. Ensure that an adequate number of qualified first-line supervisors are deployed in the field to allow supervisors to provide close and effective supervision to each officer under the supervisor's direct command, provide officers with the direction and guidance necessary to improve and develop as officers, and to identify, correct, and prevent misconduct.

11. RECRUITING, HIRING, AND PROMOTION

There are widespread concerns about the lack of diversity, especially race and gender diversity, among FPD officers. FPD should modify its systems for recruiting hiring and promotion to:

a. Ensure that the department's officer hiring and selection processes include an objective process for selection that employs reliable and valid selection devices that comport with best practices and federal anti-discrimination laws;

b. In the case of lateral hires, scrutinize prior training and qualification records as well as complaint and disciplinary history;

c. Implement validated pre-employment screening mechanisms to ensure temperamental and skill-set suitability for policing.

12. DEVELOP MECHANISMS TO MORE EFFECTIVELY RESPOND TO ALLEGATIONS OF OFFICER MISCONDUCT

Responding to allegations of officer misconduct is critical not only to correct officer behavior and identify policy, training, or tactical concerns, but also to build community confidence and police legitimacy. FPD should:

a. Modify procedures and practices for accepting complaints to make it easier and less intimidating for individuals to register formal complaints about police conduct, including providing complaint forms online and in various locations throughout the City and allowing for complaints to be submitted online and by third parties or anonymously;

b. Require that all complaints be logged and investigated;

c. Develop and implement a consistent, reliable, and fair process for investigating and responding to complaints of officer misconduct. As part of this process, FPD should:

1) Investigate all misconduct complaints, even where the complainant indicates he or she does not want the complaint investigated, or wishes to remain anonymous;

2) Not withdraw complaints without reaching a disposition;

d. Develop and implement a fair and consistent system for disciplining officers found to have committed misconduct;

e. Terminate officers found to have been materially untruthful in performance of their duties, including in completing reports or during internal affairs investigations;

f. Timely provide in writing to the Ferguson Prosecuting Attorney all impeachment information on officers who may testify or provide sworn reports, including findings of untruthfulness in internal affairs investigations, for disclosure to the defendant under *Brady v. Maryland*, 373 U.S. 83 (1963);

g. Document in a central location all misconduct complaints and investigations, including the nature of the complaint, the name of the officer, and the disposition of the investigation;

h. Maintain complete misconduct complaint investigative files in a central location;

i. Develop and implement a community-centered mediation program to resolve, as appropriate, allegations of officer misconduct.

13. PUBLICALLY SHARE INFORMATION ABOUT THE NATURE AND IMPACT OF POLICE ACTIVITIES

Transparency is a key component of good governance and community trust. Providing broad information to the public also facilitates constructive community engagement. FPD should:

a. Provide regular and specific public reports on police stop, search, arrest, ticketing, force, and community engagement activities, including particular problems and achievements, and describing the steps taken to address concerns;

    b. Provide regular public reports on allegations of misconduct, including the nature of the complaint and its resolution;

    c. Make available online and regularly update a complete set of police policies.

B. Ferguson Court Practices

1. MAKE MUNICIPAL COURT PROCESSES MORE TRANSPARENT

Restoring the legitimacy of the municipal justice system requires increased transparency regarding court operations to allow the public to assess whether the court is operating in a fair manner. The municipal court should:

    a. Make public—through a variety of means, including prominent display on the City, police, and municipal court web pages—all court-related fines, fees, and bond amounts, and a description of the municipal court payment process, including court dates, payment options, and potential consequences for non-payment or missed court dates;

    b. Create, adopt, and make public written procedures for all court operations;

    c. Collect all orders currently in effect and make those orders accessible to the public, including by posting any such materials on the City, police, and municipal court web pages. Make public all new court orders and directives as they are issued;

    d. Initiate a public education campaign to ensure individuals can have an accurate and complete understanding of how Ferguson's municipal court operates, including that appearance in court without ability to pay an owed fine will not result in arrest;

    e. Provide broadly available information to individuals regarding low-cost or cost-free legal assistance;

    f. Enhance public reporting by ensuring data provided to the

Missouri Courts Administrator is accurate, and by making that and additional data available on City and court websites, including monthly reports indicating:

1) The number of warrants issued and currently outstanding;
2) The number of cases heard during the previous month;
3) The amount of fines imposed and collected, broken down by offense, including by race;
4) Data regarding the number of Missouri Department of Revenue license suspensions initiated by the court and the number of compliance letters enabling license reinstatement issued by the court.

g. Revise the municipal court website to enable these recommendations to be fully implemented.

2. PROVIDE COMPLETE AND ACCURATE INFORMATION TO A PERSON CHARGED WITH A MUNICIPAL VIOLATION

In addition to making its processes more transparent to the public, the court should ensure that those with cases pending before the court are provided with adequate and reliable information about their case. The municipal court, in collaboration with the Patrol Division, should:

a. Ensure all FPD citations, summonses, and arrests are accompanied by sufficient, detailed information about the recipient's rights and responsibilities, including:

1) The specific municipal violation charged;
2) A person's options for addressing the charge, including whether in-person appearance is required or if alternative methods, including online payment, are available, and information regarding all pending deadlines;
3) A person's right to challenge the charge in court;
4) The exact date and time of the court session at which the person receiving the charge must or may appear;

5) Information about how to seek a continuance for a court date;

6) The specific fine imposed, if the offense has a preset fine;

7) The processes available to seek a fine reduction for financial incapacity, consistent with recommendation four set forth below;

8) The penalties for failing to meet court requirements.

b. Develop and implement a secure online system for individuals to be able to access specific details about their case, including fines owed, payments made, and pending requirements and deadlines.

3. CHANGE COURT PROCEDURES FOR TRACKING AND RESOLVING MUNICIPAL CHARGES TO SIMPLIFY COURT PROCESSES AND EXPAND AVAILABLE PAYMENT OPTIONS

The municipal court should:

a. Strictly limit those offenses requiring in-person court appearance for resolution to those for which state law requires the defendant to make an initial appearance in court;

b. Establish a process by which a person may seek a continuance of a court date, whether or not represented by counsel;

c. Continue to implement its online payment system, and expand it to allow late payments, payment plan installments, bond payments, and other court payments to be made online;

d. Continue to develop and transition to an electronic records management system for court records to ensure all case information and events are tracked and accessible to court officials and FPD staff, as appropriate. Ensure electronic records management system has appropriate controls to limit user access and ability to alter case records;

e. Ensure that the municipal court office is consistently staffed during posted business hours to allow those appearing at the court window of the police department seeking to resolve municipal charges to do so;

f. Accept partial payments from individuals, and provide clear information to individuals about payment plan options.

4. REVIEW PRESET FINE AMOUNTS AND IMPLEMENT SYSTEM FOR FINE REDUCTION

The municipal court should:

a. Immediately undertake a review of current fine amounts and ensure that they are consistent not only with regional but also statewide fine averages, are not overly punitive, and take into account the income of Ferguson residents;

b. Develop and implement a process by which individuals can appear in court to seek proportioning of preset fines to their financial ability to pay.

5. DEVELOP EFFECTIVE ABILITY-TO-PAY ASSESSMENT SYSTEM AND IMPROVE DATA COLLECTION REGARDING IMPOSED FINES

The municipal court should:

a. Develop and implement consistent written criteria for conducting an assessment of an individual's ability to pay prior to the assessment of any fine, and upon any increase in the fine or related court costs and fees. The ability-to-pay assessment should include not only a consideration of the financial resources of an individual, but also a consideration of any documented fines owed to other municipal courts;

b. Improve current procedures for collecting and tracking data regarding fine amounts imposed. Track initial fines imposed as an independent figure separate from any additional charges imposed during a case;

c. Regularly conduct internal reviews of data regarding fine assessments. This review should include an analysis of fines imposed for the same offenses, including by race of the defendant, to ensure fine assessments for like offenses are set appropriately.

6. REVISE PAYMENT PLAN PROCEDURES AND PROVIDE ALTERNATIVES TO FINE PAYMENTS FOR RESOLVING MUNICIPAL CHARGES

The municipal court should:

a. Develop and implement a specific process by which a person can enroll in a payment plan that requires reasonable periodic payments. That process should include an assessment of a person's ability to pay to determine an appropriate periodic payment amount, although a required payment shall not exceed $100. That process should also include a means for a person to seek a reduction in their monthly payment obligation in the event of a change in their financial circumstances;

b. Provide more opportunities for a person to seek leave to pay a lower amount in a given month beyond the court's current practice of requiring appearance the first Wednesday of the month at 11:00 a.m. Adopt procedures allowing individuals to seek their first request for a one-time reduction outside of court, and to have such requests be automatically granted. Such procedures should provide that subsequent requests shall be granted liberally by the Municipal Judge, and denials of requests for extensions or reduced monthly payments shall be accompanied by a written explanation of why the request was denied;

c. Cease practice of automatically issuing a warrant when a person on a payment plan misses a payment, and adopt procedures that provide for appropriate warnings following a missed payment, consistent with recommendation eight set forth below;

d. Work with community organizations and other regional groups to develop alternative penalty options besides fines, including expanding community service options. Make all individuals eligible for community service.

7. REFORM TRIAL PROCEDURES TO ENSURE FULL COMPLIANCE WITH DUE PROCESS REQUIREMENTS

The municipal court should take all necessary steps to ensure that the court's trial procedures fully comport with due process such that defendants are provided with a fair and impartial forum to challenge the charges brought against them. As part of this effort, the court shall ensure that defendants taking their case to trial are provided with all evidence relevant to guilt determinations consistent with the requirements of *Brady v. Maryland*, 373 U.S. 83 (1963), and other applicable law.

8. STOP USING ARREST WARRANTS AS A MEANS OF COLLECTING OWED FINES AND FEES

As Ferguson's own Municipal Judge has recognized, municipal code violations should result in jail in only the rarest of circumstances. To begin to address these problems, Ferguson should only jail individuals for a failure to appear on or pay a municipal code violation penalty, if at all, if the following steps have been attempted in a particular case and have failed:

a. Enforcement of fines through alternative means, including:

1) Assessment of reasonable late fees;
2) Expanding options for payment through community service;
3) Modified payment plans with reasonable amounts due and payment procedures;
4) A show cause hearing on why a warrant should not issue, including an assessment of ability to pay, where requested. At this hearing the individual has a right to counsel and, if the individual is indigent, the court will assign counsel to represent the individual. *See* Mo. Sup. Ct. R. 37.65; Mo. Mun. Benchbook, Cir. Ct., Mun. Divs. § 13.8;

b. Personal service on the individual of the Order to Show Cause Motion that provides notice of the above information regarding right to counsel and the consequences of non-appearance; and

c. If the above mechanisms are unsuccessful at securing payment or otherwise resolving the case, the court should ensure that any arrest warrant issued has the instruction that it be executed only on days that the court is in session so that the individual can be brought immediately before the court to enable the above procedures to be implemented. *See* Mo. Mun. Benchbook, Cir. Ct., Mun. Divs. § 13.8 ("If a defendant fails to appear in court on the return date of the order to show cause or motion for contempt, *a warrant should be issued to get the defendant before the court for the hearing.*") (emphasis added).

9. ALLOW WARRANTS TO BE RECALLED WITHOUT THE PAYMENT OF BOND

Ferguson recently extended its warrant recall program, also called an "amnesty" program, which allows individuals to have municipal warrants recalled and to receive a new court date without paying a bond. This program should be made permanent. The municipal court should:

a. Allow all individuals to seek warrant recall in writing or via telephone, whether represented by an attorney or not;

b. Provide information to a participating individual at the time of the warrant recall, including the number of charges pending, the fine amount due if a charge has been assessed, the options available to pay assessed fines, the deadlines for doing so, and the requirements, if any, for appearing in court.

10. MODIFY BOND AMOUNTS AND BOND AND DETENTION PROCEDURES

Ferguson has two separate municipal code bond schedules and processes: one for warrantless arrests, and another for arrests pursuant to warrants issued by the municipal court. Ferguson's municipal court recently limited the number of municipal code violations for which officers can jail an individual without a warrant, and reduced the amount of time the jail may hold a defendant who is unable to post bond from 72 to 12 hours. These changes are a positive start, but further reforms are necessary. The City and municipal court should:

a. Limit the amount of time the jail may hold a defendant unable to post bond on *all* arrests for municipal code violations or municipal arrest warrants to 12 hours;

b. Establish procedures for setting bond amounts for warrantless and warrant-based detainees that are consistent with the Equal Protection Clause's prohibition on incarcerating individuals on the basis of indigency, and that ensure bond shall in no case exceed $100 for a person arrested pursuant to a municipal warrant, regardless of the number of pending charges;

c. At the time of bond payment, provide individuals with the option of applying a bond fee to underlying fines and costs, including in the event of forfeiture;

d. Take steps necessary, including the continued development of a computerized court records management system as discussed above, to enable court staff, FPD officers, and FPD correctional officers to access case information so that a person has the option of paying the full underlying fine owed in lieu of bond upon being arrested;

e. Increase options for making a bond payment, including allowing bond payment by credit card and through the online payment system, whether by a person in jail or outside of the jail;

f. Institute closer oversight and tracking of bond payment acceptance by FPD officers and FPD correctional officers;

g. Initiate practice of issuing bond refund checks immediately upon a defendant paying their fine in full and being owed a bond refund;

h. Ensure that all court staff, FPD officers, and FPD correctional officers understand Ferguson's bond rules and procedures.

11. CONSISTENTLY PROVIDE "COMPLIANCE LETTERS" NECESSARY FOR DRIVER'S LICENSE REINSTATEMENT AFTER A PERSON MAKES AN APPEARANCE FOLLOWING A LICENSE SUSPENSION

Per official policy, the municipal court provides people who have had their licenses suspended pursuant to Mo. Rev. Stat. § 302.341.1 with compliance letters enabling the suspension to be lifted only once the underlying fine has been paid in full. Court staff told us, however, that in "sympathetic cases," they provide compliance letters that enable people to have their licenses reinstated. The court should adopt and implement a policy of providing individuals with compliance letters immediately upon a person appearing in court following a license suspension pursuant to this statute.

12. CLOSE CASES THAT REMAIN ON THE COURT'S DOCKET SOLELY BECAUSE OF FAILURE TO APPEAR CHARGES OR BOND FORFEITURES

In September 2014, the City of Ferguson repealed Ferguson Mun. Code § 13-58, which allowed the imposition of an additional "Failure to Appear" charge, fines, and fees in response to missed appearances and payments. Nonetheless, many cases remain pending on the court's docket solely on account of charges, fines, and fees issued pursuant to this statute or because of questionable bond forfeiture practices. The City and municipal court should:

a. Close all municipal cases in which the individual has paid fines equal or greater to the amount of the fine assessed for the original municipal code violation—through Failure to Appear fines and fees or forfeited bond payments—and clear all associated warrants;

b. Remove all Failure to Appear related charges, fines, and fees from current cases, and close all cases in which only a Failure to Appear charge, fine, or fee remains pending;

c. Immediately provide compliance letters so that license suspensions are lifted for all individuals whose cases are closed pursuant to these reforms.

13. COLLABORATE WITH OTHER MUNICIPALITIES AND THE STATE OF MISSOURI TO IMPLEMENT REFORMS

These recommendations should be closely evaluated and, as appropriate, implemented by other municipalities. We also recommend that the City and other municipalities work collaboratively with the state of Missouri on issues requiring statewide action, and further recommend:

a. Reform of Mo. Rev. Stat. § 302.341.1, which requires the suspension of individuals' driving licenses in certain cases where they do not appear or timely pay traffic charges involving moving violations;

b. Increased oversight of municipal courts in St. Louis County and throughout the state of Missouri to ensure that courts operate in a manner consistent with due process, equal protection, and other requirements of the Constitution and other laws.

VI. CONCLUSION

OUR INVESTIGATION INDICATES THAT FERGUSON AS A CITY HAS THE capacity to reform its approach to law enforcement. A small municipal department may offer greater potential for officers to form partnerships and have frequent, positive interactions with Ferguson residents, repairing and maintaining police-community relationships. *See, e.g.,* Jim Burack, *Putting the "Local" Back in Local Law Enforcement, in, American Policing in 2022: Essays on the Future of the Profession* 79–83 (Debra R. Cohen McCullough & Deborah L. Spence, eds., 2012). These reform efforts will be well worth the considerable time and dedication they will require, as they have the potential to make Ferguson safer and more united.

NOTES

II. Background

1. *See* 2012 Census of Governments, U.S. Census Bureau (Sept. 2013), available at http://factfinder.census.gov/bkmk/table/1.0/en/COG/2012/ORG13 .ST05P?slice=GEO~0400000US29 (last visited Feb. 26, 2015).

2. *See* 2010 Census, U.S. Census Bureau (2010), available at http://factfinder .census.gov/bkmk/table/1.0/en/DEC/10_SF1/QTP3/1600000US2923986 (last visited Feb. 26, 2015).

3. *See* 1990 Census of Population General Population Characteristics Missouri, U.S. Census Bureau (Apr. 1992), available at ftp://ftp2.census.gov/library/ publications/1992/dec/cp-1-27.pdf (last visited Feb. 26, 2015).

4. *See* Race Alone or in Combination: 2000, U.S. Census Bureau (2000), available at http://factfinder.census.gov/bkmk/table/1.0/en/DEC/00_SF1/ QTP5/1600000US2923986 (last visited Feb. 26, 2015).

5. 2010 Census, supra note 2.

6. *See* Poverty Status in the Past 12 Months 2009–2013 American Community Survey 5-Year Estimates, U.S. Census Bureau (2014), available at http://factfinder .census.gov/bkmk/table/1.0/en/ACS/13_5YR/S1701/1600000US2923986 (last visited Feb. 26, 2015).

7. This is evidenced not only by FPD's own records, but also by Uniform Crime Reports data for Ferguson, which show a downward trend in serious crime over the last ten years. *See Uniform Crime Reports*, Federal Bureau of Investigation, http:// www.fbi.gov/about-us/cjis/ucr/crime-in-the-u.s (last visited Feb. 26, 2015).

III. Ferguson Law Enforcement Efforts Are Focused on Generating Revenue

8. Each of these yearly totals excludes certain court fees that are designated for particular purposes, but that nonetheless are paid directly to the City. For example,

$2 of the court fee that accompanies every citation for a municipal code violation is set aside to be used for police training. That fee is used only by the City of Ferguson and is deposited in the City's general fund; nonetheless, the City's budget does not include that fee in its totals for "municipal court" revenue. In 2012 and 2013, the police training fee brought in, respectively, another $24,724 and $22,938 in revenue.

9. FPD's financial focus has also led FPD to elevate municipal enforcement over state-law enforcement. Even where individuals commit violations of state law, if there is an analogous municipal code provision, the police department will nearly always charge the offense under municipal law. A senior member of FPD's command told us that all Ferguson police officers understand that, when a fine is the likely punishment, municipal rather than state charges should be pursued so that Ferguson will reap the financial benefit.

10. After a recommendation we made during this investigation, Ferguson has recently begun a very limited "correctable violation" or "fix-it" ticket program, under which charges for certain violations can be dismissed if corrected within a certain period of time.

11. Katherine Smith, *Ferguson to Increase Police Ticketing to Close City's Budget Gap*, *Bloomberg News* (Dec. 12, 2014), http://www.bloomberg.com /news/articles/2014-12-12/ferguson-to-increase-police-ticketing-to-close -city-sbudget-gap.

12. Ferguson officials have asserted that in the last fiscal year revenue from the municipal court comprised only 12% of City revenue, but they have not made clear how they calculated this figure. It appears that 12% is the proportion of Ferguson's *total* revenue (forecasted to amount to $18.62 million in 2014) derived from fines and fees (forecasted to be $2.09 million in 2014). Guidelines issued by the Missouri State Auditor in December 2014 provide, however, that the 30% cap outlined in Mo. Rev. Stat. § 302.341.2 imposes a limit on the makeup of fines and fees in *general* use revenue, excluding any revenue designated for a particular purpose. Notably, the current 30% state cap only applies to fines and fees derived from "traffic violations." It thus appears that, for purposes of the state cap, Ferguson must ensure that its traffic-related fines and fees do not exceed 30% of its "General Fund" revenue. In 2014, Ferguson's General Fund revenue was forecasted to be $12.33 million.

IV. Ferguson Law Enforcement Practices Violate the Law and Undermine Community Trust, Especially Among African Americans

13. FPD policy states that "[o]fficers should document" all field contacts and field interrogation "relevant to criminal activity and identification of criminal

suspects on the appropriate Department approved computer entry forms." FPD General Order 407.00. Policy requires that a "Field Investigation Report" be completed for persons and vehicles "in all instances when an officer feels" that the subject "may be in the area for a questionable or suspicious purpose." FPD General Order 422.01. In practice, however, FPD officers do not reliably document field contacts, particularly of pedestrians, and the department does not evaluate such field contacts.

14. FPD officers are not consistent in how they label this charge in their reports. They refer to violations of Section 29-16 as both "Failure to Comply" and "Failure to Obey." This report refers to all violations of this code provision as "Failure to Comply."

15. Other broad quality-of-life ordinances in the Ferguson municipal code, such as the disorderly conduct provision, may also be vulnerable to attack as unconstitutionally vague or overbroad. *See* Ferguson Mun. Code § 29-94 (defining disorderly conduct to include the conduct of "[a]ny person, while in a public place, who utters in a loud, abusive or threatening manner, any obscene words, epithets or *similar abusive language*") (emphasis added).

16. The ordinance on interfering with arrest, detention, or stop, Ferguson Mun. Code § 29-17, does not actually permit arrest unless the subject uses or threatens violence, which did not occur here. Another code provision the officer may have relied on, § 29-19, is likely unconstitutionally overbroad because it prohibits obstruction of government operations "in any manner whatsoever." *See Hill*, 482 U.S. at 455, 462, 466 (invalidating ordinance that made it unlawful to "in any manner oppose, molest, abuse, or interrupt any policeman in the execution of his duty").

17. This set, however, did not include any substantive information on the August 9, 2014 shooting of Michael Brown by Officer Darren Wilson. That incident is being separately investigated by the Criminal Section of the Civil Rights Division and the U.S. Attorney's Office for the Eastern District of Missouri.

18. ECWs have two modes. In dart mode, an officer fires a cartridge that sends two darts or prongs into a person's body, penetrating the skin and delivering a jolt of electricity of a length determined by the officer. In drive-stun mode, sometimes referred to as "pain compliance" mode, an officer presses the weapon directly against a person's body, pulling the trigger to activate the electricity. Many agencies strictly limit the use of ECWs in drive-stun mode because of the potential for abuse.

19. The Ferguson-Florissant School District serves over 11,000 students, about 80% of whom are African American. *See* Ferguson-Florissant District Demographic Data 2014 & 2015, Mo. Dep't of Elementary & Secondary Educ., http://mcds.dese.mo.gov/guidedinquiry/Pages/District-and-School-Information.aspx (last visited Feb. 26, 2015).

20. The influence of revenue on the court, described both in Part II and in Part III.B. of this Report, may itself be unlawful. *See Ward v. Vill. of Monroeville*, 409 U.S. 57, 58–62 (1972) (finding a violation of the due process right to a fair and impartial trial where a town mayor served as judge and was also responsible for the town's finances, which were substantially dependent on "fines, forfeitures, costs, and fees" collected by the court).

21. As with many of the problematic court practices that we identify in this report, other municipalities in St. Louis County also have imposed a separate Failure to Appear charge, fine, and fee for missed court appearances and payments. Many continue to do so.

22. As discussed in Part II of this report, City officials have acknowledged several of these procedural deficiencies. In 2012, a City Councilmember, citing specific examples, urged against reappointing Judge Brockmeyer because he "often times does not listen to the testimony, does not review the reports or the criminal history of defendants, and doesn't let all the pertinent witnesses testify before rendering a verdict."

23. This finding of untruthfulness by a police officer constitutes impeachment evidence that must be disclosed in any trial in which the officer testifies for the City. Under the Fourteenth Amendment, the failure to disclose evidence that is "favorable to an accused" violates due process "where the evidence is material either to guilt or to punishment, irrespective of the good faith or bad faith of the prosecution." *Brady v. Maryland*, 373 U.S. 83, 87 (1963). This duty applies to impeachment evidence, *United States v. Bagley*, 473 U.S. 667, 676 (1985), and it applies even if the defendant does not request the evidence, *United States v. Agurs*, 427 U.S. 97, 107 (1976). The duty encompasses, furthermore, information that should be known to the prosecutor, including information known solely by the police department. *Kyles v. Whitley*, 514 U.S. 419, 437 (1995). This constitutional duty to disclose appears to extend to municipal court cases, which can result in jail terms of up to three months under Section 29-2 of Ferguson's municipal code. *See City of Kansas City v. Oxley*, 579 S.W.2d 113, 114 (Mo. 1979) (en banc) (holding that the due process standard of proof beyond a reasonable doubt applied in a municipal court speeding case because "the violation has criminal overtones"); *see also City of Cape Girardeau v. Jones*, 725 S.W.2d 904, 907–09 (Mo. Ct. App. 1987) (explaining that reasonable doubt standard applied to municipal trespass prosecution because municipal ordinance violations are "quasi-criminal," and reversing two convictions based on privilege against self-incrimination). We are aware of at least two cases, from January 2015, in which the City called this officer as a witness without disclosing the finding of untruthfulness to the defense.

24. *See City Courts*, City of Ferguson, http://www.fergusoncity.com/60/The -City-Of-Ferguson-Municipal-Courts (last visited Feb. 26, 2015). By contrast,

the neighboring municipality of Normandy operates a court website with an entire page containing information regarding fine due dates, methods of payment, and different payment options, including the availability of payment plans for those who cannot afford to pay a fine in full. *See How Do I Pay a Ticket/Fine?*, City of Normandy, http://www.cityofnormandy.gov/index.aspx?NID=570 (last visited Feb. 26, 2015).

25. Prior to September 2014, a second missed court appearance (or a single missed payment) would result not only in a warrant being issued, but also the imposition of an additional Failure to Appear *charge*. This charge was imposed automatically. It does not appear that there was any attempt by the court to inform individuals that a failure to appear could be excused upon a showing of good cause, or to provide individuals with an opportunity to make such a showing. Additionally, just as the court does not currently send any notice informing a defendant that an arrest warrant has been issued, the court did not send any notice that this additional Failure to Appear charge had been brought.

26. The email reports that the defendant, a black male, was booked into jail. This email does not provide the full context of the circumstances that led to the 10-day jail sentence and further information is required to assess the appropriateness of that order. Nonetheless, the email suggests that the court jailed a defendant for refusing to answer questions, which raises significant Fifth Amendment concerns. There is also no indication as to whether the defendant was represented or, if not, was allowed or afforded representation to defend against the contempt charge and 10-day sentence.

27. While Missouri provides a process to secure a temporary waiver of a license suspension, we have heard from many that this process can be difficult and, in any case, is only available in certain circumstances.

28. By initiating the license suspension procedure after a single missed appearance and without first providing notice or an opportunity to remedy the missed appearance, the court appears to have violated Missouri law. *See* Mo. Rev. Stat. § 302.341.1 (providing that after a missed appearance associated with a moving violation, a court "shall within ten days . . . inform the defendant by ordinary mail at the last address shown on the court records that the court will order the director of revenue to suspend the defendant's driving privileges if the charges are not disposed of and fully paid within thirty days from the date of mailing").

29. *See City Courts*, City of Ferguson, http://www.fergusoncity.com/60/The-City-Of-Ferguson-Municipal-Courts (last visited Feb. 26, 2015); *Ferguson Municipal Court*, Your Missouri Courts, http://www.courts.mo.gov/page.jsp?id=8862 (last visited Feb. 26, 2015).

30. Recently, the court has allowed some individuals over age 19 to resolve

fines through community service, but that remains a rarity. *See City of Ferguson Continues Court Reform Initiative by Offering Community Service Program*, City of Ferguson (Dec. 15, 2014), http://www.fergusoncity.com/CivicAlerts .aspx?AID=370&ARC=699 (stating community service program was launched in partnership with Ferguson Youth Initiative in February 2014 "to assist teenagers and certain other defendants").

31. As stated in the Missouri Municipal Court Handbook produced by the Circuit Court: "Defendants who fail or refuse to pay their fines and costs can be extremely difficult to deal with, but if there is a credible threat of incarceration if they do not pay, the job of collection becomes much easier." Mo. Mun. Benchbook, Cir. Ct., Mun. Divs. § 13.6 (2010).

32. Ferguson officials have also told us that the arrest warrant is issued not because of the missed payment per se, but rather because the person missing the payment failed to abide by the court's rules. But the Supreme Court has rejected that contention, too. In *Bearden*, the Court noted that the sentencing court's stated concern "was that the petitioner had disobeyed a prior court order to pay the fine," but found that the sentence nonetheless "is no more than imprisoning a person solely because he lacks funds" to pay. *Bearden*, 461 U.S. at 674.

33. Additionally, Ferguson's municipal code provides: "When a sentence for violation of any provision of this Code or other ordinance of the city . . . includes a fine and such fine is not paid, or if the costs of prosecution adjudged against an offender are not paid, the person under sentence shall be imprisoned one day for every ten dollars ($10.00) of any such unpaid fine or costs . . . not to exceed a total of four (4) months." Ferguson Mun. Code § 1-16. Our investigation did not uncover any evidence that the court has sentenced anyone to imprisonment pursuant to this statute in the past several years. Nonetheless, it is concerning that this statute, which unconstitutionally sanctions imprisonment for failing to pay a fine, remains in effect. *Cf. Bearden v. Georgia*, 461 U.S. 660, 671 (1983).

34. In December 2014, the court set forth a bond schedule for warrantless arrests, which provides that, for all but 14 code violations, a person arrested pursuant to a municipal code violation and brought to Ferguson City Jail shall be issued a citation or summons and released on his or her own recognizance without any bond payment required. For those 14 code violations requiring a bond, the court has set "fixed" bond amounts, although these are subject to the court's discretion to raise or lower those amounts at the request of the City or the detained individual. The court's recent order further provides that, even if an individual does not pay the bond required, he or she shall in any case be released after 12 hours, rather than the previous 72-hour limit.

35. For example, the recent orders fail to specify that, in considering whether to adjust the bond imposed, the court shall make an assessment of an individual's

ability to pay, and assign bond proportionately. *Cf. Pugh v. Rainwater*, 572 F.2d 1053, 1057 (5th Cir. 1978) (en banc) (noting that the incarceration of those who cannot afford to meet the requirements of a fixed bond schedule "without meaningful consideration of other possible alternatives" infringes on due process and equal protection requirements).

36. The court's website states that the court window is open from 8:30 a.m. to 5:00 p.m., not 4:00 p.m. *See City Courts*, City of Ferguson, http://www.fergus oncity.com/60/The-City-Of-Ferguson-Municipal-Courts (last visited Feb. 26, 2015).

37. Critically, however, when a person attends court after paying a bond and is assessed a fine, court staff members *do* automatically apply the bond already paid to the fine owed, and in fact require application of the bond to the fine regardless of the defendant's wishes. Thus, the court has simultaneously asserted that it *can* apply a bond to a fine without a defendant's consent when the bond would otherwise be returned to the defendant, but that it *cannot* apply a bond to a fine without a defendant's consent when the bond would otherwise be forfeited into the City's own accounts.

38. As noted above, FPD charges violations of Municipal Code Section 29-16 as both Failure to Obey and Failure to Comply. Court data carries forward this inconsistency.

39. While there are limitations to using basic population data as a benchmark when evaluating whether there are racial disparities in vehicle stops, it is sufficiently reliable here. In fact, in Ferguson, black drivers might account for *less* of the driving pool than would be expected from overall population rates because a lower proportion of blacks than whites is at or above the minimum driving age. *See 2009–2013 5-Year American Community Survey*, U.S. Census Bureau (2015) (showing higher proportion of black population in under-15 and under-19 age categories than white population). Ferguson officials have told us that they believe that black drivers account for *more* of the driving pool than their 67% share of the population because the driving pool also includes drivers traveling from neighboring municipalities—many of which have higher black populations than Ferguson. Our investigation casts doubt upon that claim. An analysis of zip-code data from the 53,850 summonses FPD issued from January 1, 2009 to October 14, 2014, shows that the African-American makeup for all zip codes receiving a summons—weighted by population size and the number of summonses received by people from that zip code—is 63%. Thus, there is substantial reason to believe that the share of drivers in Ferguson who are black is in fact lower than population data suggests.

40. Assessing contraband or "hit rates" is a generally accepted practice in the field of criminology to "operationaliz[e] the concept of 'intent to discriminate.'"

The test shows "bias against a protected group if the success rate of searches on that group is lower than on another group." Nicola Persico & Petra Todd, *The Hit Rates Test for Racial Bias in Motor-Vehicle Searches*, 25 Justice Quarterly 37, 52 (2008). Indeed, as noted below, in assessing whether racially disparate impact is motivated by discriminatory intent for Equal Protection Clause purposes, disparity can itself provide probative evidence of discriminatory intent.

41. As noted above, African Americans received 90% of all citations issued by FPD from October 2012 to July 2014. This data shows that 86% of people receiving citations following an FPD traffic stop between October 2012 and October 2014 were African American.

42. It is generally accepted practice in the field of statistics to consider any result that would occur by chance less than five times out of 100 to be statistically significant.

43. Similar to the post-stop outcome disparities—which show disparities in FPD practices after an initial stop has been made—these figures show disparities in FPD practices after a decision to issue a citation has been made. Thus, these disparities are not based in any part on population data.

44. Although the state-mandated racial profiling data collected during traffic stops captures ethnicity in addition to race, most other FPD reports capture race only. As a result, these figures for non-African Americans include not only whites, but also non-black Latinos. That FPD's data collection methods do not consistently capture ethnicity does not affect this report's analysis of the disparate impact imposed on African Americans, but it has prevented an analysis of whether FPD practices also disparately impact Latinos. In 2010, Latinos comprised 1% of Ferguson's population. *See 2010 Census*, U.S. Census Bureau (2010), *available at* http://factfinder.census.gov/bkmk/table/1.0/en/DEC/10_SF1/QTP3/1600000US2923986 (last visited Feb. 26, 2015).

45. The universe of cases in this and subsequent analyses consisted of cases filed in 2011 because, given that some cases endure for years, a more recent sample would have excluded a greater amount of data from case events that have not yet occurred.

46. The ten offenses or offense categories analyzed include: 1) Manner of Walking in Roadway; 2) Failure to Comply; 3) Resisting Arrest; 4) Peace Disturbance; 5) Failure to Obey; 6) High Grass and Weeds; 7) One Headlight; 8) Expired License Plate; 9) aggregated data for 14 different parking violation offenses; and 10) aggregated data for four different headlight offenses, including: One Headlight; Defective Headlights; No Headlights; and Failure to Maintain Headlights.

47. Ferguson's discriminatory practices also violate Title VI and the Safe Streets Act, which, in addition to prohibiting some forms of unintentional conduct that

has a disparate impact based on race, also prohibit intentionally discriminatory conduct that has a disparate impact. *See* 42 U.S.C. § 2000d; 42 U.S.C. § 3789d.

48. Social psychologists have long recognized the influence of implicit racial bias on decision making, and law enforcement experts have similarly acknowledged the impact of implicit racial bias on law enforcement decisions. *See, e.g.*, R. Richard Banks, Jennifer L. Eberhardt, & Lee Ross, *Discrimination and Implicit Bias in a Racially Unequal Society*, 94 Cal. L. Rev. 1169 (2006); Tracey G. Gove, *Implicit Bias and Law Enforcement*, The Police Chief (October 2011).

49. We did find one instance in 2012 in which the City Manager forwarded an email that played upon stereotypes of Latinos, but within minutes of sending it, sent another email to the recipient in which he stated he had not seen the offensive part of the email and apologized for the "inappropriate and offensive" message. Police and court staff took no such corrective action, and indeed in many instances expressed amusement at the offensive correspondence.

50. We were able to review far more emails from FPD supervisors than patrol officers. City officials informed us that, while many FPD supervisors have their email accounts on hard drives in the police department, most patrol officers use a form of webmail that does not retain messages once they are deleted.

51. Richard Rothstein, *The Making of Ferguson*, Econ. Policy Inst. (Oct. 2014), *available at* http://www.epi.org/publication/making-ferguson/.

52. *See Missouri Vehicle Stops Report*, Missouri Attorney General, http://ago .mo.gov/VehicleStops/Reports.php?lea=161 (last visited Feb. 13, 2015).

53. Data for the entire state of Missouri shows an even higher "Disparity Index" for those years than the disparity index present in Ferguson. This raises, by the state's own metric, considerable concerns about policing outside of Ferguson as well.

54. Although beyond the scope of this investigation, it appears clear that individuals' experiences with other law enforcement agencies in St. Louis County, including with the police departments in surrounding municipalities and the County Police, in many instances have contributed to a general distrust of law enforcement that impacts interactions with the Ferguson police and municipal court.

55. This incident raises another concern regarding whether a second-hand informal account of a complaint, often the only record Ferguson retains, conveys the seriousness of the allegation of misconduct. In this illustrative instance, our conversation with a witness to this incident indicates that the officer pointed his weapon at each employee as he spoke to him, and threatened to shoot both, despite knowing that they were simply employees taking out the trash.

56. We found additional examples of FPD officers behaving in public in a manner that reflects poorly on FPD and law enforcement more generally. In November 2010, an officer was arrested for DUI by an Illinois police officer who found his

car crashed in a ditch off the highway. Earlier that night he and his squad mates—including his sergeant—were thrown out of a bar for bullying a customer. The officer received a thirty-day suspension for the DUI. Neither the sergeant nor any officers was disciplined for their behavior in the bar. In September 2012, an officer stood by eating a sandwich while a fight broke out at an annual street festival. After finally getting involved to break up the fight, he publically berated and cursed at his squad mates, screamed and cursed at the two female street vendors who were fighting, and pepper-sprayed a handcuffed female arrestee in the back of his patrol car. The officer received a written reprimand.

57. While the Chief's "log" of Internal Affairs ("IA") investigations contains many sustained allegations, most of these were internally generated; that is, the complaint was made by an FPD employee, usually a commander. In addition, we found that a majority of complaints are never investigated as IA cases, or even logged as complaints. The Chief's log, which he told us included all complaint investigations, includes 56 investigations from January 2010 through July 2014. Our review indicates that there were significantly more complaints of misconduct during this time period. Despite repeated requests, FPD provided us no other record of complaints received or investigated.

58. FPD may have initially accepted this as a formal complaint, but then informally withdrew it after completion of the investigation. No rationale is provided for doing so, but the case does not appear on the Chief's IA investigation log, and another case with this same IA number appears instead.

59. Our review of FPD's handling of misconduct complaints is just one source of our concern about FPD's efforts to ensure that officers are truthful in their reports and testimony, and to take appropriate measures when they are not. As discussed above, our review of FPD offense and force reports also raises this concern.

60. While the emphasis in Ferguson has been on racial diversity, FPD also, like many police agencies, has strikingly disparate gender diversity: in Ferguson, approximately 55% of residents are female, but FPD has only four female officers. *See* 2010 *Census*, U.S. Census Bureau (2010), *available at* factfinder.census.gov/bkmk/table/1.0/en/DEC/10_DP/DPDP1/1600000US2923986 (last visited Feb. 26, 2015). During our investigation we received many complaints about FPD's lack of gender diversity as well.

61. While not the focus of our investigation, the information we reviewed indicated that Ferguson's efforts to retain qualified female and black officers may be compromised by the same biases we saw more broadly in the department. In particular, while the focus of our investigation did not permit us to reach a conclusive finding, we found evidence that FPD tolerates sexual harassment by male officers, and has responded poorly to allegations of sexual harassment that have been made by female officers.